Growing Up
the Greek Way
in the
Big Apple

Growing Up the Greek Way in the Big Apple

Mike Pappas

iUniverse, Inc.
Bloomington

Growing Up the Greek Way in the Big Apple

iUniverse books may be ordered through booksellers or by contacting:

iUniverse
1663 Liberty Drive
Bloomington, IN 47403
www.iuniverse.com
1-800-Authors (1-800-288-4677)

Because of the dynamic nature of the Internet, any web addresses or links contained in this book may have changed since publication and may no longer be valid. The views expressed in this work are solely those of the author and do not necessarily reflect the views of the publisher, and the publisher hereby disclaims any responsibility for them.

Any people depicted in stock imagery provided by Thinkstock are models, and such images are being used for illustrative purposes only.

Certain stock imagery © Thinkstock.

ISBN: 978-1-4620-0069-2 (sc)
ISBN: 978-1-4620-0071-5 (dj)
ISBN: 978-1-4620-0070-8 (ebook)

Printed in the United States of America

iUniverse rev. date: 03/18/2011

Contents

Acknowledgments

———◦———

I dedicate this book to my family—to my father, who gave me an early jump start in life and died when I was just starting to get my feet wet, and my mother, who raised us all to be responsible and guided me to what I am today.

To my brother Jack, who was always looking into the future but was not quite able to finish his goal.

To my brother Harry, who was more like a father to my sisters and me as we were growing up. To this day, I still look at him as more than just a brother.

To my sister Tessie, who worried about everybody and everything as we were all growing up, and still does today.

To my sister Mary, who always complained about everything but has a good heart.

You all touch my life in many ways.

I remember all we went through, the good and tough times, together. I love you all.

And, of course, to my wife, Moska, who helped me raise three wonderful sons—Charles, John, and Michael—and who helped me through some hard times. I also especially want to thank my son Michael, who encouraged me in writing this book. I love you all.

I want to thank Father Bill Gikas from my parish, St. George Greek Orthodox Church of Hamilton, New Jersey, for his spiritual assistance on "Journey through Holy Week."

Introduction

———◆———

Time Waits for Nobody

One thing I will say is that time waits for nobody. If you do not use the time to act now, you may look back and be sorry to have never made the effort.

When I retired, I found I was still getting up early. So I decided to write a book on all my years in the food business. I titled the book *Thirty-Five Years of Bologna*.

I still think about the days when I was growing up, like it was just yesterday.

Chapter 1

You're Only Young Once

My parents came to America when Europe was on the brink of war. Just like all immigrants, they were seeking the American dream.

I was born in the 1940s. We started out on the east side in Midtown Manhattan, in a four-room apartment on the top floor of a five-floor walk-up. We were fortunate that we had a bathroom in the apartment, because many had to share one with others.

I had two older brothers and two younger sisters. Mom and Dad had the old-fashioned tradition and spoke only Greek while we were all growing up.

Dad was tall and thin. He was particularly firm in some things, yet, he was pretty easygoing in other ways.

Mom was a "super mom"; she was on the short side but was a giant in our eyes. She had a heart of gold and would go out of her way to satisfy people. Mom had lost a child, which left her with a physical problem. She required an operation to correct it, but, as she was not too fond of hospitals, she kept postponing it. She would wear a support to keep her problem from getting worse.

With most Greek families

then, it was most crucial that the children be named after their parents, grandparents, uncles and aunts.

I briefly remember when I was about five years old; I took money from my mother's purse. I had no real understanding of the value of money. I took some of my friends to the neighborhood candy store and bought them all types of snacks.

I remember the clerk giving me all these other bills. He allegedly told one of my brothers. My father gave me a spanking that to this day, I can still remember. I learned a vital lesson: if you want money, you better earn it.

I can vaguely remember Dad talking about when President Truman announced on the radio the successful bombing of Japan. Then shortly after, people were celebrating the end of the war in the streets. It was not until years later that I learned it was an atomic bomb. I have some memories of the blackouts, when the city was in total darkness in case of an enemy attack, just at the end of World War II.

When I was about six years old, I enjoyed going shopping with Mom at the different stores. Mom would leave my sisters home with Dad when he was off. She would shop at different department stores; her favorite was Bloomingdale's. She would purchase everything there, from towels to furniture. Every month, she made her payment of ten dollars. She never missed a payment, no matter how lousy things were. Mom did not even trust mailing it; she either went in person herself or sent one of us to pay it when we got older.

I especially enjoyed riding on the Third Avenue el. The fare was just five cents, and they gave out free transfers.

One day, I grabbed a transfer slip. I wanted to surprise my aunt and uncle who lived outside the city in Maspeth, Queens. The transfer slip was valid for only four hours from the time they issued it. I did not have much time. I told Mom I was going to go out and play. Mom's favorite comment was *"Ta matia sou dekatesita,"* which translates, (Have fourteen eyes).

So I went on my way to experience the pleasure of traveling on the New York City Subway to see my aunt and uncle. The reason I loved going to their house was they had a television. To make watching it more enticing, they would put this glass shield over the TV screen to make it colored. It would also magnify the picture, but the problem was everything was blue on top and green on the bottom.

Having gone with my parents before, I remembered the front lights on the train were a specific color, indicating the train's destination. I was sure I knew the way, But when I got off the train, everything looked strange. I saw a sign that read, "Flushing." It was then I realized that something was not right. I was not sure what to do, so I stuck my hands into my pockets and pulled out two cents. I realized I did not have enough money to get back on the train.

I kept on walking, hoping I would see something I recognized. Now I was starting to get a little frightened.

I remembered my father always telling me if ever I ran into a problem or got lost, I should look for a policeman. Well, one found me; he saw me alone and came up to me. He asked me where my parents were, and I told him I was trying to find my aunt and uncle's house. He asked me where they lived; I told him I did not know their address, but I knew what the house looked like. I remember he laughed.

He took me to the Flushing police station. We went back to where the policemen would hang out. They gave me all different types of junk food; I was thinking to myself that getting lost was like a party.

I was afraid, not knowing what to expect, but I was also having a fabulous time playing games with some of the policemen. They asked me if I knew my telephone number and address. I told the policeman, who was sitting behind his desk, that we had no telephone, but I knew my home address. They were able to get the telephone number of the drugstore that was downstairs in the apartment house. I remember they had a black cat that I would play with. Shortly after, they told me that they had gotten ahold of my family and someone was coming to get me.

A short time later, my brother Jack came. When he got there, they asked me if he was even my brother. Though Jack was only fourteen, he looked older. When we left, he said I was in trouble; after hearing that, I was afraid to go home. I got a well-deserved spanking and got grounded from various activities for a long time. After that episode, my parents kept a closer watch on me.

Mom never trusted us when we washed up; she would wash our hair, especially on Saturday night. We had this wash basin in the kitchen where she would scrub our hair using a brush. The more we complained, the harder she scrubbed.

When we all sat down to eat, especially when we had company, it was vital for all of us to be properly dressed. The men and boys would always wear a shirt with a necktie, and the women and girls wore dresses with no exceptions. One would think we were going to church the way we had to dress. Whether we liked it or not, we all learned at a young age that you do not argue with "Greek traditions."

Mom would scold us whenever we did not finish eating. She always told us to be thankful for what was on our plates, because in other parts of the world, people were starving. I would tell Mom they could have what I did not want or finish. That did not go over too well, and she would scold me for talking out of line.

The only time we drank soda was on Sunday and festive occasions, if we behaved. We were such fanatics that we would measure the level in the glass with a ruler just to make sure we did not get cheated.

I always sat in the corner when we ate. I was a fast eater, and I would always finish first, forcing my sisters, especially Mary, to move, and of course, she would always complain.

I also had this problem after I would eat. I was always running to the bathroom. With seven of us, and just one bathroom, it was a problem. It was always a headache trying to get done every morning, especially having three females under one roof.

Mom loved to look out the window and just take in the scenery. As we were living on the top floor, her view went as far as her eyes could see. Mom would lay a blanket on the windowsill just to be comfortable. She would do this mainly because she could watch us and keep us in check.

When we were young, we were not allowed to cross the street unless supervised. Tessie called Mom so she could watch her cross the street to play with some other friends. Mom gave her the okay that it was safe to cross. While she was crossing the street, out of nowhere, this car made an illegal turn. Seeing this, Mom was almost ready to jump out the window when the car hit her. Tessie went to the hospital to be sure that everything was all right. Mom was always a worrier, but this episode made her even worse.

A family portrait was a must in our parents' eyes. So we all had to get dressed up as if we were going to church. I will never forget the photographer

earned his wages that day. We were all so out of control, between Mary crying and my brothers and I laughing. Tessie was the only one who somewhat behaved.

We were lucky the pictures came out right, because the way we behaved, our parents were just about ready to kill us.

There were times when we all would go visiting. We had no say in the matter, but we would make the most of it. When we got a little older, we did not go as often.

A "name day" was a bigger occasion for celebration than birthdays when it came to many Greek families. Only the man of the household had this celebration.

I remember my father's, but I particularly remember when it was any of our uncles. There were so many different foods and drinks. I never saw so many relatives and friends in one house at one time as I did at a name day celebration. It was also customary to pull the ear of the person who was celebrating this day.

Mom would make these honey puffs (*loukamades*) especially on this occasion. I would watch her while she was taking them out of the deep fryer. She would then put honey, powdered sugar, and cinnamon on them as a finishing touch. I would sneakily grab one and burn my mouth, and she would shout, *"Ka la nasuepopses!"* which translates, ("You get what you deserve.")

I also noticed that as our parents and relatives passed on, this function slowly disappeared.

Mom and Dad were extremely strict and would not tolerate any inappropriate behavior. Let's just say the method that they used would put parents in jail today. Not that I totally agree with their methods of discipline, but I will say that we all just stayed within their standards.

Mom would send me to the store. One day, she sent me after napkins. It was Sunday, and the supermarkets and local grocery stores were not open because of a blue law, so I went to the local Whelan's Drugstore on Forty-Second Street.

I could not seem to find napkins, and the female clerk asked me what I needed. I said, "Napkins."

She said, "Sanitary?"

I responded, "I guess."

She put them in a bag. I gave her money, took my change, and headed home.

I gave my mother the bag; she reached in and started laughing. *"Vhef, vlocker!"* ("Hey, stupid!"), she said. "What is this?"

"I told the lady at the drugstore I wanted some napkins, and she gave me them. I thought the package looked different."

She sent me back, and I told the woman they were the wrong napkins. She laughed, too, and then said, "We don't sell those napkins." Then she gave me the money back.

Knowing we needed napkins, I stopped at a restaurant to acquire some. I looked around, and when it was clear, I grabbed a handful.

When I got home, I told my mother they did not sell regular napkins, but I borrowed some from the restaurant. She laughed at me and said, *"Ve gel'eft"* ("You thief.")

The milkman would come almost every morning and deliver the milk. It came in glass quart bottles with a two-inch foam of cream on top; we had to shake it before we drank it. Now that was milk!

Other times, when Mom needed a few items to hold her until she did her main shopping, she would send me to the local grocery store. I always enjoyed going. Why? It had its rewards.

Most of the time, I would also treat myself to either a Devil dog, Hostess Chocolate Cupcakes, a Drake's Coffee Cake, or a pickle; they were just five cents each. Sometimes my mother caught me when I had left evidence of chocolate on the side of my mouth.

We even had a *bakalko* (a Greek grocery store) nearby. Many times, when Mom needed something specific that could not be found at the local grocery store, I would go shopping there.

They had all different types of Greek items and cheeses. The owner would give me a sample every time I went shopping there. The thing that stood out was the salted sardines they sold loose from this huge can. Both my mother and father loved to snack on them with some Greek bread, olives, and, of course, their wine.

Mom would buy wine by the gallon, and if I remember correctly, she would buy either Gallo or Manischewitz. For as long as I could remember, while we were eating supper, she would keep it on the floor by her side and have a glass or two.

When any one of us would come back from shopping, she would have to ask for the change back, especially me. Mom may not have graduated, but when it came to the money, you could not fool her.

I would see signs at the grocery store and blasted all over the neighborhood on the trolleys/buses and subway stations about a beauty contest for "Miss Rheingold Beer." I would always get excited knowing I could vote, though it was illegal because of my age. I would run to other stores, grabbing as many ballots as I could without getting in trouble or getting caught. I think more people voted for Miss Rheingold than they did for the local politicians.

All the girls were pretty. It was hard to decide on just one, so I would vote for all of them. The way I looked at it, whoever won had my vote.

In the 1940s, after the war, many food items, like sugar, coffee, and bread, were available only in limited amounts per family. My brothers and I would all go to the store and buy these items, especially bread, because one loaf was never enough.

Whenever Mom would be looking for any of us, she would call out our names, sometimes so loudly that everybody on the block heard it, just in case we did not. She was as smart as a fox; she knew if we did not hear her, we were not where we belonged. We always tried to come up with a reasonable excuse; whether she believed us or not was another story.

The neighborhood had a fire department just down the street, and I still remember the station number: Engine 21. I would many times hang out there just so I could watch the firemen cleaning their fire trucks and equipment and sometimes training.

Mom never wanted me to hang around there, mainly because she felt I did not belong there and I might hurt myself. So when she was busy with her household chores, I would sneak out. Somehow, she always knew where I was; she always had one of my brothers come get me. She would yell and even use the broom on me for not listening. I sometimes thought she had "Greek radar." It got to the point I would hide the broom, so she could not use it on me.

Whenever any one of us got sick, we had a doctor come to us. Being Greek, we had a Greek doctor; his name was Doctor Toni's. Hard to believe, a doctor made house calls and was at the house within hours of your call!

We had no phone, so we had to go downstairs to the local drugstore, which was called Seinfeld's, and use the phone there. Sometimes, it was not open, so we would go to the local bar, which was called Liberty and was right around the corner. It always seemed to be available. Mom always kept nickels handy especially for this purpose.

I would enjoy having to use the phone at the Liberty bar. They had a television, and I remember this one evening, they were watching boxing; Rocky Marciano won the heavyweight title, and all the customers went crazy.

Most of the time, when we would have sore throats or even something else, Dr. Toni's cure was a single dash of iodine. He would ask one of us for an unsharpened pencil; he would put a piece of cotton on the tip, and then he would dip it in iodine and put it in our mouths and coat the tonsils. We'd all had it done many times, so we knew the awful aftertaste it left. Like magic, the next morning, we were back on our feet, and our sore throat or whatever ailment disappeared.

All the times we all got sick over the years, Mom was always there to nurse us back to health. I can't remember Mom ever getting sick; if she did, we never knew.

The druggist (pharmacist) was like a friend to most of the people in the neighborhood. If ever we got something in our eyes or a splinter, he was always there to remove the foreign matter. Believe me when I say I was in there many times, for one reason or another.

Summer came, and school was out. The weather would get hot, and the only relief we could get was by going to the beach. We had no air conditioner, and even if we could have afforded one, the old wiring would not have been able to take the load.

Many people would sit out on their fire escapes just to get some relief from the heat. Since our apartment was on the corner, we would get a cross draft. The unfortunate part was it was a hot one, so many times, we would go to Coney Island or Brighton Beach to chill off. As rewards, if we behaved, we could go on some of the rides afterward. Sometimes, we got a treat and had Nathan's hot dogs with all the fixings.

I was always mesmerized by all the rides at Coney Island; my favorite rides were the whip and the scooter carts. I went on the giant roller coaster once, and I was so scared my hairs were sticking up. Call me a "chicken," but that was the first and last time I ever went on that ride.

Mom always brought this gargantuan blanket whenever we went to the beach. She would make her own cover to protect us from the direct sunlight. One day, I wandered off and fell asleep in the sun unprotected. Little did I know at the time, but I caught a serious case of sunstroke. Mom had a fit when she saw how red I had gotten. She said I was going to be sorry that I had wandered off.

Mom's prediction was so accurate. That night, I was bedridden, and they had to call the doctor. After the doctor had examined me, he prescribed a particular medication. I hated taking any medication. The pills were the size of a quarter, and I would not take them. I would hide them under my pillow. After a couple of days, I was not showing any improvement, and everyone was getting concerned.

They called the doctor to tell him I was not showing any improvement. He was at the house within hours. He examined me but could not understand why I was not showing signs of improvement. Dad was even getting upset with the doctor because of that. I could hear the doctor telling my parents, "Be sure he is taking all the medicine."

Mom was changing my sheets and found the pills hidden under my covers. I could hear the anger in her voice. Both my father and mother scolded me and told me if I wanted to get better, I had to take my medicine. I said, "Did you see the size of them?" So Mom cut them into smaller pieces. She stood there and made sure I swallowed them. Just to be sure, she even double-checked my mouth.

I had this nightmare; it was really dark, and I felt the heat coming off my body. I saw this older woman all dressed in black. She was leaning over me making strange sounds and moving this clear glass over my head. It felt like I could not move, and I thought I'd died and gone to hell.

That morning, I woke up like a new person. I told everybody about my awful dream. They all laughed and said that it was no dream. They said Aunt Harriet had been there, and she was using some Greek witchcraft. She was a tremendous believer in witchcraft. After this, we had second thoughts about her witchcraft. I will always wonder how I got better!

Mom was always concerned about us staying healthy, and she would give us all a spoonful of cod-liver oil. It had the worst taste you could imagine, and I would hide it just so I would not have to take it. For me, it was always a no-win situation; Mom always won.

One day, I saw my mother doing something that piqued my curiosity. She removed her teeth from her mouth and put them in a glass filled with water. I was trying to remove my teeth, not knowing any better. Mom saw me; I told her, "I am trying to remove my teeth as you do."

She said, "Don't be silly," and explained to me how vital it was "to take care of your teeth." Mom told me, "If you leave them alone, they will go away, just like mine did." I made sure from then on that I took brushing my teeth seriously.

Mom had to purchase a new mattress for us; with three of us sleeping in one bed, it was wearing out that much faster. I removed the tag, unaware of the warning on it, and my brothers said I was going to jail. They said, "Didn't you read what the label says? It says, 'Do not remove under plenty of law.'" For the longest time, I believed them, and every time I saw a policeman, I thought he was going to arrest me.

Mom was a fanatic when it came to keeping the house in order. When Mom was not cooking, she was cleaning. If it would not clean up, she would paint it. Sometimes the kitchen had three different shades of paint. In her eyes, it was better than looking dirty. We would laugh and tease Mom because when she painted, she would wear these overalls. We told her she looked like a neighbor who always wore overalls or she looked like a truck driver.

When Mom got upset with any of us, she had a cute way of expressing it. She would take her right hand and close it tight. Then she would say to "*feesur*" ("blow") on her hand, and then she would open her hand and say, "Na." This was her way of calling us stupid or silly.

As we were growing up, we were always told to greet our elders in a courteous manner. We would call a woman, "*Thea,*" which means "aunt," and a man, "*Theo*," which means "uncle." So I one day, I asked Dad how come we had so many aunts and uncles.

He replied, "We don't; it is a matter of respect."

When I was young, when the Christmas season was getting close, I tried to be more obedient. I always wondered how Santa came into the house, because we had no fireplace. My father told me that Santa would make a hole in the ceiling and come in that way. It sounded legit because we lived on the top floor. For years, I believed it because there were cracks in the ceiling that looked like someone had tried to fix it.

I always looked forward to going to the Macy's parade mainly to see Santa. I could not wait to see him and give him my Christmas list. Did you know that Santa made his first showing at Macy's as far back as 1870? Dad told me that in Greece, a beggar was traditionally given the first piece of bread from the Christmas loaf.

As the years rolled on, I became more curious about how Santa came into the house. One Christmas Eve, I decided to stay awake. I saw my father and mother putting the gifts under the tree. I was somewhat disappointed, but I just pretended, mainly because my sisters still believed.

I will never forget the blizzard we had just after Christmas in 1947. It was the worst snowstorm you could ever imagine. We had about twenty-six inches in just one day. The city was shut down, and nothing was moving. The best was there was no school for almost a week after the Christmas holidays.

Everybody was stranded; we could not even get out of the apartment house, because the snowdrifts were over ten feet high. Some people had to dig a tunnel through the snow if they wanted to get out.

They finally started plowing the streets after it stopped snowing. There was so much snow they ran out of places to put it. The only solution was to truck it to the East River.

I wanted to go out, but Mom would yell at me and say, "Come to your senses; the snow is much too deep." So I had no choice but to wait a few days until some of it melted.

I wanted to go out and play, but Mom would always tell me, "No." When I was finally able to go outside, Mom prepared me as if I was going to the North Pole. She put this heavy, thick sweater on me; it had once been one of my brothers. I remember it had this piece of thread hanging, and it was annoying me. So I started pulling the loose thread. I just kept pulling on it, and it kept getting longer. It was not until I saw half of the sweater had disappeared that I realized what I'd done.

Mom had a fit when she saw the sweater. She shouted, "Your brothers wore this for years, and in just one day, you ruined it." As usual, she scolded me. Another lesson I learned while I was growing up: be careful what you pull.

Mom loved it when it snowed; she said it killed any germs or bacteria in the air. Now, every time it snows, I think about what she said.

There were many mornings we woke up to no heat. I also remember Mom using a large metal spoon to bang on the radiators when we had no heat. It must have worked, because shortly thereafter, the heat would be back. Then there were times when it was so hot it was like being in a steam room.

Every New Year, Mom would make lentil soup, which I never ate. She also made this sweet bread called *Vasilopita*, which was a tradition for the Greek families. It was also customary to put a coin into the bread and then cut it into pieces for all members of the family, oldest first, with a piece for the house. Whoever got the piece with the coin had exceptional luck for the new year.

We would search for it and get crumbs all over the table and floor. Mom would shout at us for making a mess. If the piece for the house got it, we all got upset, but Dad said that meant good luck for everyone. There are other stories; this is what I remembered.

My brothers and some of their friends would go to the YMCA every Saturday morning bright and early, and sometimes, they would take me.

Mom felt I was too young to hang around with the older guys. I would plead with her, and she would eventually give in. Mom was smart; she knew how much I looked forward to going, and she would use this to punish me if I did not behave.

We would work out and play with the medicine ball. The ball was almost as high as I was tall. Later, we would go running around the track a few times. I enjoyed going into the steam room after we did all the workouts. Then we would go swimming and then take a shower. Mom would always make sure I was still in one piece when I came home.

On the way home, we would stop at the penny arcades on Broadway, where for a dime, we could play many games. I got hooked on playing, so a bunch of my friends and I would go pretty regularly. When they raised the price to a nickel and a dime, we could not afford to go as often.

While I was growing up, I made many new friends. I had made friends with this older man who happened to be a chef in the local tavern. It was tremendously convenient, especially when supper was not ready. This was the same place we would call the doctor from when the drugstore was not open. He would give my friend Lou and me a turkey drumstick or some rare roast beef through the backyard window. Maybe this was the reason I got hooked and still love them.

He had told us when he got to the point where he could no longer support or feed himself, we would help him. I always remembered that comment he made. So whenever I would see someone who needed a helping hand, whether they were elderly or young, I would go the extra few steps to help them.

Chapter 2

My Holy Side

Every Saturday night and on certain holidays, Mom would always "bless" the house with the *Thimiata* (holy scents). When we got older, we would take turns doing it. The scent was so overpowering, it left the apartment smelling just like a church.

Sunday and most holidays, we all went to church together. We would take the bus uptown to the Holy Trinity Greek Cathedral on Seventy-Fourth Street.

Mom was like the mailman; neither rain nor snow could stop her. Mom always went early, because in her eyes, she had to be there before the Gospel reading. She even had a "particular" seat she always sat in, so if it was a "special" service, she would leave that much earlier—without us if we were not ready—just to be sure she had her seat.

When it came to the holidays like Christmas but especially Easter, church was always packed. Where were all these people during a regular Sunday service? During Holy Week or the Christmas services, they would "reserve" the section in which Mom usually sat. Well, that did not go over too well with Mom; her arguments were, "Where are these people during the rest of the year?" Mom wondered why she should give up her seat for a high-society parishioner who came only during the holiday and festive occasions. They knew she was correct in her feelings and gave her that respect. One comment I can make about Mom is she always spoke her mind.

During the holy period of Easter (Lent), we were not allowed to eat any meat or dairy products. So since our parents were from the old country, they followed the faith religiously. Mom would not even purchase those items, much less have them in the house. I would ask her, "Are you trying to starve us?" because the icebox was just about empty. She would scold me like only a mother could and say it was Lent, and we all should give thanks to "our Lord" and stop complaining.

For forty days during Lent, Mom would make all these different vegetarian meals. She would also make a lentil soup, which was a tradition, especially during this period. The rule was whatever Mom made, that was what we would eat. If you did not want it, you did not eat.

My problem was that many of the meals she made did not look appetizing to me, so I would let my eyes do my thinking. I would make myself a mustard sandwich, just to have something to eat. There were many times I went to bed without eating, and again, she would scold me for that.

It did not stop there; some days, especially during Holy Week, the radio was off-limits. We would try to sneak and listen to the radio on low volume, but Mom had ears like a hawk. She would scold us by saying, "*Throw-pea*" (Shame on you), and turn it off and even unplug it.

I will always remember going to the Saturday midnight Resurrection services at a fairly young age. Just at midnight, the lights were turned off. The priest came with a lit candle and started singing, "*Thevte Lavete Fos*" (Come Receive the Light). Then he passed the light on to others until everybody had a lit candle. Then, just after midnight, the Resurrection of Christ was proclaimed with the words, "Christ is Risen." In Greece, the lit candle would have been sent from Jerusalem to celebrate the Resurrection.

My brother Jack was a regular altar boy, and Harry would fill in at times. Everyone left early except Harry and me, so they could sit at their usual place. We went later and sat in the rear of the church. Within minutes, it got so crowded we could just about not move.

At one service, I was feeling terrific about having my own lit candle. A few minutes later, Harry said, "I smell something burning." We both looked around, and sure enough, the woman in front of me had her hair on fire. Not realizing, I had held my candle too close to her hair.

We started to try to put it out by hitting her head. We told the woman, and she started screaming. Everybody stopped and looked. We finally put the fire out; I am sure the hair spray on her hair did not help.

When the collection tray was being passed, I tried to hold it, but I dropped it, and all the money, mostly coins, fell on the ground, making a loud noise. Everybody turned to look. Harry wanted to hide.

We would all receive Holy Communion during this "holiest" of all holidays. We sometimes went on Thursday morning, but because of school, we'd usually go on Saturday mornings. As religious as our parents were, they felt school was too valuable to miss.

This is the very "Body and Blood of Holy Christ." We had to go to confession, which was to cleanse our souls. Since it was Lent, we were already fasting, but the day came to receive Holy Communion and we could not eat or drink anything until we received Communion.

Mom always said we must follow and do what was expected of us correctly before taking Holy Communion.

During the period of Lent, Mom would do a lot of baking for Easter Sunday. Mom had everything planned out. She would bake while we were in school; this way, nobody would bother her. Mom was as slick as a fox; she would hide the finished products. Our favorite was a butter cookie called *"Koulourakia"*.

Since my brothers were altar boys, Mom wanted me to get involved at a young age; she felt it would keep me out of trouble. So I became an altar boy at the age of seven. I remained an altar boy until I was in my teens.

Whenever Archbishop Athenagoras came to church for services, it seemed he always had me under his wings. I would stand under his long, grayish beard while he was standing at his special chair. Mom thought that it was an honor to be that close to him; as for me, I found it extremely uncomfortable, especially with his long, itchy beard.

He was the Archbishop from 1931 to 1948; he was then sent to Constantinople (Istanbul), Turkey, where he became patriarch and remained so from 1948 to 1972. Archbishop Michael was enthroned in 1948 to 1958. It was an honor to see him do the invocation at the inauguration of the thirty-fourth president, Dwight Eisenhower, to his second term on January 21, 1957. It was a first ever done by an Orthodox hierarch. Another nifty aspect of being an altar boy was being close to everything.

During a service, we were all on our knees praying when something caught my attention. I suddenly saw this gold feather slowly descending from above. I carefully observed it as it landed on my arm. At that moment, I was not sure what to do, so I removed it from my arm and put it in my shirt pocket.

My first instinct was that it had come from an angel from up above. Being an altar boy, I felt close to my church, but after seeing this, I felt even more attached.

I told my mother about the "gold feather" that had landed on my arm. She said to me, "Come to your senses." I pulled it out of my shirt pocket and showed it to her.

Jack heard this and said, "Hey, stupid, it's gold paint that peeled off the church ceiling that was recently painted."

Mom laughed. Even though, he might have been right, I still felt deep down that it was from an angel, so I kept it. Since I was an altar boy, Mom always made sure I attended each of the services during Holy Week.

Mom always volunteered me for the altar whenever they needed me. Starting with Palm Sunday services, the church would do a full week of religious services, and each one had a distinct meaning, which lead in to Easter Sunday (*Pasca*).

A Journey through Holy Week

Saturday of Lazarus
In Bethany, about two miles from Jerusalem, Jesus raised His friend Lazarus from the dead as a prelude to His own Resurrection. At many churches, after the Divine Liturgy, children are invited to make crosses out of the palm branches for the next day's celebration of Palm Sunday.

Palm Sunday
Palm Sunday celebrates the glorious and triumphal feast of the entrance of Jesus into Jerusalem. Zechariah had prophesied the entrance of the Messiah into the holy city of Jerusalem. A custom of distributing blessed palm branches in the form of crosses to the people in the church prevails to this day, commemorating the triumphal entry of Christ as King of kings and the ushering in of His eternal heavenly kingdom.

On Palm Sunday evening, upon entry into the church, you immediately encounter the icon of Christ as "the Bridegroom." This special icon will remain at the front of the church for the three days of Bridegroom services. Christ is the Bridegroom in that He has taken the Church as His bride, and according to scripture, as Bridegroom, He enters the marriage feast (heaven) to which we are all invited if we are vigilant and prepared in this life. In the scriptural readings, we read that Christ curses the fig tree; it withers and dies, showing His divine power over creation. He is triumphant and powerful, as well as loving and forgiving. During this solemn Bridegroom service, the faithful express their anticipation of Jesus' Second Coming by holding a lit candle.

Holy Monday
The readings describe certain Sanhedrin (high Hebrew council leaders), who were enemies of Jesus, confronting Him and trying to trap Him with His own radical ideas. Jesus outsmarted them, skillfully answering their questions and making them look foolish, which only enraged them more. Then Jesus turned the tables on the Jewish leaders, calling them hypocrites because they

told people to observe traditions without following such themselves. These events set the stage for the Jewish leaders' plot to have Jesus arrested for trying to overthrow the Roman rulers in Jerusalem.

Holy Tuesday

We hear the story of the sinful woman in the Gospel of Luke, which teaches us what we must do to choose a life of good over one of sin. This woman sat at Jesus' feet, weeping for her sins, and anointed Him with expensive ointment. When she met Jesus, she saw a better way to live and wanted to change.

Holy Wednesday—Holy Unction

It is the evening of repentance, confession, and the remission of sins by the Lord. Holy Unction is the cleansing of sins and the renewing of the body and the spirit of the faithful through the special healing prayers and the blessing of oil. Holy Unction is one of the seven major sacraments of the Church. At the end of the service, the priest anoints the people with holy oil, the visible carrier of the grace of God and His healing powers.

Holy Thursday Morning

Christ shares salvation with us, uniting us to Him in one sacramental moment. Here we join Him in the upper room, where He offers the first Eucharist (Thanksgiving to God). This was the Passover meal, where he sat for the last time with His disciples. Later, He washed their feet as a sign of humility and servant leadership. Jesus showed His love for each of them and how He loves each of us through His sacrifice on the cross. During the Divine Liturgy, Holy Communion, the very Body and Blood of Christ is offered to the faithful.

Holy Thursday Evening

This is a long service where the "Twelve Gospels" are read. According to the narrative scriptures, Jesus knew He was going to die, which brought Him intense sorrow. He asked His Father to take the "cup" or sacrifice of His life away, but then yielded and said, "not what I will, but what You will," because He is both divine and human and, as the Son of God, obedient to the Father.

It is okay to feel a little antsy or tired and have your feet hurt. Remember the pain and suffering He endured for all mankind (humankind) on this day.

Holy Friday Afternoon

When we come to church on this day, we are attending the descent from the Cross and the burial of our Lord and Savior Jesus Christ. When Jesus' friend,

Joseph of Arimathea, removed the body of Jesus from the cross, he anointed it with oil and then "wrapped it in a clean linen shroud and laid it in his own new tomb." This event is reenacted by the priest at this service.

Holy Friday Evening
This service is filled with melodies and customs that are many hundreds of years old. The faithful chant the lamentations at Jesus' burial. The church is filled with flowers especially on the decorated *Epitaphios* (the tomb of Christ). There is a long procession around the outside of the church (when the weather is nice). Everybody holds a lit candle and sings many solemn hymns.

I remember, as a youngster, I, along with my brothers and sisters, would traditionally crawl under the *Epitaphios* to show our love for all His suffering and pain while recalling all He had done for all mankind.

Holy Saturday Morning
Christ had been crucified and buried. His remaining eleven disciples scattered—Judas, who betrayed Jesus, had hung himself after he realized what he had done. On this day, we read these prophecies. One story is of Jonah, who was swallowed into the belly of a fish and remained there for three days before being spit out; this is a prelude to Jesus' three days in the tomb and subsequent Resurrection. Another story is from the book of Daniel. It is about three young men who were thrown into a fiery furnace because they refused to worship the Babylonian king. Even while they were in the furnace, they continued praising God, and because of their faithfulness, they were not burned. For this, we sing a hymn to connect these three youths to our Lord's three days in the tomb. Also during the Liturgy, Holy Communion is offered to all. The priest commemorates Jesus' descent into Hades (the place of death) by singing a triumphal hymn, "Arise O God and Judge the Earth," while joyfully scattering laurel leaves all over the church.

Holy Saturday Evening
This is the celebration service we all waited for. This is the most joyful moment of our Christian lives. Just at midnight, we celebrate Jesus Christ risen from the dead, victorious over death. Later, we continue by celebrating the Divine Liturgy. Holy Communion is offered to all, and everyone proclaims and sings, "Christ is Risen." The faithful greet each other for forty days thereafter by saying, "Christ is Risen," and responding with, "Truly He is Risen!"

Easter Sunday
This is the vespers service of Agape (Love) where the Paschal Gospel is proclaimed in many different languages, first by the priest and then by the

faithful people. This is the only day in the Greek Orthodox calendar when the nonordained (laity) can proclaim the Gospel in Church, as usually it is the clerics' privilege to do so. People bring their decorated Paschal candles to be lit with the Light of the Resurrection again on this day.

It is customary to bring home the "Easter candle" lit. Mom would keep the light burning as long as possible. She would keep it where she had all the "icons" that she kept in her bedroom.

The hardest part was getting the lit candle home without it going out, and if the weather was inclement, it made it even more difficult. So we all would bring a lit candle home, which almost guaranteed one of us would be successful.

We would get many stares from people for carrying the lit candles especially on the bus.

After the midnight services, we would go home and start the first part of the Easter feast. Mom would leave shortly before us, so she could prepare everything. By the time, we started eating, it was like two o'clock in the morning. Mom would make this recipe called *Mageritsa* (Easter soup), made from organs of the lamb, like the intestines, the liver, the stomach, and the heart. It does not sound appetizing, but it was tasty. Call me crazy, I would eat this, and yet with many other meals, I would just walk away from the table.

I remember Harry's fiancée Lilly checking it out for the first time, with hesitation. When she found out what the ingredients were, that quickly ended her desire to eat it. That was okay, because that meant more for me, because I could never have enough.

Mom, for years, was able to get the ingredients from the local butcher with no problems. Then the FDA banned them from the market. In order to continue making it, Mom had no choice but to buy the ingredients from "the black-market butcher." We would tease her about that.

We would all get a few hours' sleep, except for Mom. She was up at the crack of dawn doing her "last-minute" cooking. We always wondered where she got this energy.

Then came the Easter Sunday dinner; after fasting for well over forty days, it was not surprising how we all looked forward to this time.

Mom would dye the eggs on Holy Thursday, and all the eggs were red. Red represented the color of Jesus' blood, which was shed at the cross.

We would first crack the eggs, which was traditional. The egg represented the tomb of Christ. The cracking of the egg symbolized Christ breaking the seal of this tomb. The one who succeeded without having his or her egg cracked was blessed with luck.

Days before and even that morning, Mom would be cooking up a storm. Mom made things like *Spanakopita* (spinach and feta in fillo), *Tiropetakia* (feta cheese in fillo), *Pastitsio* (meat and macaroni casserole), *Dolmathes* (stuffed grape leaves with rice), and *Keftethes* (fried meatballs), plus the lamb, roast beef, and different styles of potatoes and rice, and different kinds of vegetables and salad—not to mention the bread.

There was always so much food there was not ever enough space on the table for everything. We would feast like there was no tomorrow.

Later, Mom would bring out all the baked goods like the *Tsoureki* (sweetbread), *Loukamades* (honey puffs), *Kourambiethes* (almond shortbread), *Baklava* (fillo-nut pastry), and of course, our favorite of all: the *Koulourakia* (butter cookies).

Even though we were all stuffed from all the constant eating, we still had room for all the sweets.

I can remember from when we were really young to even after we all got married, Easter was one of the biggest holidays we celebrated as a family.

Mom and Dad would go the extra mile to be sure we all had new clothing for Easter Sunday. Mom would get all of us new clothing and new shoes; she would check the newspaper for the best sales.

She would drag us all downtown to stores like Kline's on Fourteenth Street (on the square) and buy my brothers and me new suits and my sisters new dresses.

Easter (Pasca) is celebrated after the Western churches, mainly because we followed the Old Eastern Orthodox calendar. Every few years, it would fall on the same Sunday. I remember it was the first full moon during the Jewish Passover.

The fun part was because we celebrated it later, we were able to buy the Easter candy at half price.

Mom and Dad loved cheese. When it was Lent, Mom did not keep cheese in the icebox. Over the years, I developed a taste for cheese. Mom loved this one cheese that my sisters always said smelled like dirty feet. I would have a habit of always finishing up the blue cheese that she enjoyed. She loved it in the morning on her toast.

Mom knew I was the culprit because my sisters hated cheese and my brothers were not true cheese eaters like me. She would yell at me, because I would always eat it all up. At one point, she had to hide it in the icebox. She disguised it by wrapping it in something I did not want. Now I know where I get my shrewdness.

Mom got us all involved in Sunday school, so we could learn more about our faith. I came to meet my friend Gregg there. We were not troublemakers, but we would always have the same habit of changing the subject from religion to other topics.

Both our mothers came down on us when they found out we were disrupting the class session. I do not know whose was worse; all I know was my mother told me I better behave, or I was going to pay in other ways. I always wondered what she meant with that remark!

Chapter 3

Still Growing Up

Mom got us all involved in the Greek Independence Day Parade. The celebration was on March 25, and for one reason or another, they would have the parade about a month later. Do not ask why, because I always asked why, and I always got a different answer every time. Mom was enthusiastic about this mainly because of Greece's independence from the Turks, under whose rule they'd lived for over four hundred years.

The parade first stepped off in 1951 with different churches and organizations from all over the tri-state. Some even took a greater part in this glorious celebration. Over twenty-five thousand marched in it and more than a hundred thousand watched it firsthand, not to mention the thousands who saw it on TV.

The parade would start at about Sixty-First Street, just off Central Park, and we would walk uptown on Fifth Avenue. It would pass the Greek archdiocese on Seventy-Ninth street and continue past the Greek Cathedral where it ended.

When the weather was sunny and mild, it was always a pleasure to walk, but when the weather was inclement, that was a different story.

My friends always teased me when I wore the traditional Greek evzone outfit in the parade. Either way, I always enjoyed and got a tremendous thrill from marching in the parade.

In the latter years of the fifties, my cousin Athena, with whom I grew up, won the honor of being Junior Miss Greek Independence and would be in the parade.

I always looked forward to going to the Ringling Brothers and Barnum& Bailey Circus, known as the "Greatest Show on Earth." It was held in the old Madison Square Garden. Often, the only reason I went was because my godmother took me. She always called it a belated birthday gift.

My biggest thrill was after the circus, when we went to the sideshows to see all those strange attractions. I would also take advantage and would eat so much junk food, because Mom was not one to keep any snacks on hand.

My godmother always bought me a souvenir, but this one year, she bought me this live lizard instead. She at first hesitated about buying it, especially without my mother knowing anything about it. I knew Mom would never let me have it, so I had no choice but to keep it a secret from her. I kept it in my room in this distinctive box while I was at school.

A few days later, it managed to get out of the box. It seems while Mom was eating her lunch, it somehow got on the kitchen table, and she freaked out. She threw a pot at it, knocking it onto the ground. She then flushed it down the toilet.

I guess that is what I get for keeping it a secret. The stranger's thing years later, in the mid fifties a lizard-type monster called Godzilla was revealed.

Living in an apartment house had its drawbacks. As much as Mom tried to keep the apartment clean, we had a serious problem with bugs (roaches). When the light was turned on, they would take off in different directions. No matter what Mom did, it was a no-win situation. Many times, they appeared out of paper grocery bags when Mom came home from shopping.

Bugs were not the only problem we encountered; we had our share of mice. Sometimes at night, we could hear them. Dad always planted traps, but no sooner than we caught one, others appeared. Just like with the bugs, it was like a no-win situation. This was the main reason why Mom would get upset with anyone who left any food or crumbs on the floor or table.

Someone had told me as I was growing up that there were more mice and rats living in the city than people. That sent a chill through me. Then I also learned that there were more two-legged rats moving around us than the other species. At first, I did not catch on, but as I got older, I got the message.

Mom got us all enrolled in Greek school at the church we attended. I guess school and homework were not enough; we had to rush to get to Greek school. It made for a long and tiring day.

Growing up in those years, discipline was a key factor, and there was no getting around it. During Greek school, there were days when I misbehaved and the teacher would literally take a wooden stick ruler and hit my hands. Sometimes, he hit my hand so hard the wooden ruler broke. Even the principal, whom we called "Sharkie," would come into the classroom and observe. He would sit in the back and do the same if he felt the situation warranted it.

Mom and Dad felt this method of discipline was to their satisfaction when we were out of hand. Maybe they were right, because I would think twice about doing something stupid again—not that I did not try to do it again.

My brothers, on occasion, would play hooky and go to a movie right across the street. When I found out, I decided to try it. I tried it once, and I got caught. They got mad at me because I made it much more difficult for them.

Every night after supper, one of us would run downstairs to buy the newspaper. There was the *Daily Mirror*, but our favorite was the *Daily News*, which was only two cents. Then we would argue over the comics.

My favorite comics were *Joe Palooka, Henry, Li'l Abner, Smilin' Jack*, and *Orphan Annie*. There were others, like *Mickey Finn, Kerry Drake, Brenda Starr, Winnie Winkle, Henry*, and of course *Louie*. My most favorite was *Dick Tracy*. I would follow each episode. It was like it was a fix. Mom would tell me I should study as much as I read the comics.

I got involved in saving comic books like Batman and Robin, Superman, Tarzan the Ape Man, Captain Marble, and my favorite, Tales from the Crypt. The first comic book was introduced in America in 1934.

I also saved baseball cards, like Jackie Robinson, Joe DiMaggio, Yogi Berra, Whitey Ford, Mickey Mantle, Babe Ruth, and many others.

My friends would put their baseball cards in the spokes of their bikes to make a rubbing sound, like a motor, but not me, I took care of mine. To keep them clean and in excellent condition, I would wrap them as well as some of my comic books in wax paper. When Mom needed the wax paper, all she found was an empty box. She would yell and say, "*Sockleters!*" ("Nonsense!").

I enjoyed collecting them and hoped maybe someday they might be worth something. I had to hide the baseball cards and the comics, because Mom had a habit of throwing them in the trash.

My sister Tessie, years later, worked for a company called Dunhill that sold pipes and other expensive products. Every so often, when they had a clearance sale, she would bring many different styles of pipes home.

Mom hated anything related to smoking, so when Tessie brought any of them home, she would try to throw them out. I told her that I was collecting them and had no intention of smoking them. Mom was a neat freak and hated any clutter. She shouted, "Do we not have enough *scopether* in the house?" (*Scopether* means "junk.")

The unfortunate part was years later, while I was in the service, before she moved, she got rid of everything. Mom could not understand why I got terribly upset.

Mom was not too crazy about escalators. Whenever we took the subway, she always used the stairs or the elevator. It did not matter how long the walk was, she would never use the escalators. If you've ever used the Flushing line subway station, from Forty-Second Street off Third Avenue, you would know how long and steep the walk was. It was surprising how she did it all those years.

I came to find out years earlier she'd had a mishap on an escalator. It scared her so badly she would never ride on one again. One observation about Mom, she never gave things like that a second chance.

Mom would go and visit some relatives or friends. There were times I did not go, and she would give me a small task. My brothers were either working or had somewhere to go, so that left just me.

Her biggest concern was that the water tray from the bottom of the icebox be emptied. She kept repeating that I might forget. We were all emptying the tray on a regular basis. I will never forget this one-day, Mom had gone shopping early. After she completed her chores, she went visiting with my sisters. Again, she said, "Be sure to empty the water tray and wait for the iceman before you go out to play."

As usual, I said, "Stop worrying." I lucked out because the iceman came early.

I had emptied the tray earlier, so I did not have to do it for a while. I was out all day and lost track of time. Did I mention it was also the middle of the summer? When I walked into the kitchen, there was water all over the floor. I had not thought about it, but because of the heat and humidity, the ice was melting faster. What a mess! I was lucky no one was home. So I got the mop and cleaned up the mess. I said to myself, "Now, no one will ever know about the flood."

After I had cleaned up the disaster, I sat down, relaxed, and started listening to the radio. I was reading a comic book. Later, my Mom came home with my sisters, and soon after, my brothers arrived. I was thinking to myself I had certainly lucked out.

Later that night, there was a knock at the door followed by the doorbell. My first thought was that it was dad and that he had forgotten his key. Oops! It was the neighbor from below us. All we heard was the neighbor screaming at Mom. Everybody but me ran to see what had happened.

She had just gotten home and said part of her ceiling had come down because of some water that had leaked through her ceiling. All I could hear was my name being repeated. I wanted to try to hide. Mom's Greek temper was at its max; she wanted to kill me.

I tried to deny it. All I could say was, "We have to get an electric icebox, because this would never have happened. Most of my friends have one. How come we do not have one?"

Mom was so angry she took the broom to hit me. I ran into the bathroom and locked the door. With the broom in her hand, she yelled at me for being careless. Mom had a short fuse, but also a forgiving heart. That was her character.

Mom still had her doubts, but in many cases, she never had any choices. If I wanted to win back her trust, I had to be it sure that it did not happen again. I would empty the tray more often, so it would not happen again.

It took a while, but we finally got an electric icebox. Thank goodness, no more emptying the water tray and no more icemen to worry about. My brother Jack reminded me it was not called an electric icebox but a "refrigerator."

Mom would wash all the clothes by hand using this old, worn-out washboard, and then she would hang them on the roof, which we called the "tar beach," because when it was hot and sunny, the tar on the roof got as hot as sand on the beach. It also made it a lot easier and much more convenient living on the top floor.

We would take turns bringing the clothes down when they were dry, and believe me, on a hot day, they dried fast. Mom would even hang clothes in the winter as long as it was sunny.

One Saturday, when it was on the cold side, she asked me to bring down the clothes before it got dark, because she was going visiting. As usual, I went out to play and totally forgot about the clothes. It was already dark. I got a flashlight and went to get the clothes.

Since I was short, I sometimes had to jump to reach the clothes. This one day, I found they had frozen and stuck to the clothesline and on some of the shirts, the sleeves were standing straight up. Now I was afraid that they would break in half. I carefully removed the pieces of clothing one by one. How would I explain this? I had a real problem because Mom had warned me.

I turned on the oven hoping to defrost them before Mom got back. Just my luck, they came home sooner than I thought; all I could do was just turn off the oven, throw all the clothes onto the bed, and shut the door. Later that night, Mom asked where the clothes were. I said, "They're on my bed." She told my sisters to take care of the clothing. My sisters started shouting that the clothes were all cold and damp. Mom looked at me, said I did not listen, and scolded me about it.

Sometimes when it rained, Mom would hang some clothing on a clothesline in the kitchen. When the bedroom door was open, I had a clear view. I would imagine all types of things like ghosts and shadows. If we had lightning and thunder at night, I would hide under my blankets. Was I reading too many comics or seeing too many movies?

Then we got this manual washing machine that would save time, because it did not require scrubbing the clothes. Years later, they provided a coin-operated washing machine and dryer in the cellar. This made it easier for Mom, and believe me, I loved the feeling, too.

We had our share of hoboes in the neighborhood; many times, they would sleep under the stairs in the apartment house. They were always looking for a handout. Mom would always yell at me when I tried to help them. I felt sorry for them, and sometimes, when I took the trash down, I would give them the food I did not eat.

My brothers and I were always fighting over stupid things. One day, Harry grabbed my hand and stuck it onto the hot radiator and held it. I screamed and fought him off, but not before he left me with a scar that I have to this day. I can still see it. All I can say is he left me with a lasting impression. Mom and Dad asked Harry why he burned my hand. He simply said, "I just felt like it, because maybe he deserved it."

Harry sometimes got stuck with me, when everybody was out for one reason or another. I remember going to what was once called Horn & Hardart's, the automatic, on Forty-Second Street and Third Avenue, which was only a few blocks from where we lived. (For those who don't know what an automatic is, it is a coin-operated, self-service restaurant.)

We were somewhat mischievous while we were growing up. So when we went to the automatic, we did silly thinks like loosen the tops of the sugar, salt, and pepper shakers and put salt in the sugar shaker.

My favorite was putting water on the seats. We would go upstairs to the

balcony and watch the people using the salt, pepper, and sugar. We watched as they got mad and upset when they used them, especially when the top would fall off. The best was when they felt their wet seats after they sat down. What we did was mean, but at that time, we called it clean fun.

We would speak in Greek to each other and make jokes about the people around us. There was this one day, a busboy was cleaning the tables, and we were talking and making jokes about him. The joke was on us, though, because he was Greek, and he came back at us. Another lesson in life is: be careful what you say, because you never know who is listening.

I remember my first encounter with the public. I was just turning seven years old. My father bought me a shoe-shine box for my birthday, mainly because I always enjoyed shining his shoes that he wore for work.

Dad worked as a waiter at the Commodore Hotel on Forty-Second Street near Grand Central Terminal. When the weather was pleasant, I would occasionally walk with him; it was a short walk.

Dad had long legs, and he would walk quickly, so I had to walk faster to keep up with him. While we were walking, "he would talk to me about important things".

He told me I needed to understand the difference between right and wrong, and if I made a mistake, I should admit it. Most important, I should always stand up for what I believe and use common sense. Follow those basic rules, he said, and you will make and live a better life.

Dad was always prompt. When he said a certain time, he was always there. It must have rubbed off on me. There were many things I learned from Dad, and punctuality was one of them.

During our walks, I saw some older men shining shoes, and they were making money. All of sudden, I saw nickels flashing in front of my eyes. I was thinking, *I have a shoe-shine box. What else do I need to start my own little business?*

So after carefully thinking out my plans, I decided to sneak out after school. First, I would finish my homework, and then I would go to where Dad worked and find a spot.

My first day of doing business was a tough one. The other shoe-shine men would yell at me because I was in their territory. So I had to move to another location, and I was chased away again. I said to myself, "Business is extremely difficult to start." With all the moving around, I was not making any money. So I went home without making a nickel.

The doorman at the hotel saw me the next day and noticed the other shoe-shine men were chasing me away and shouting at me. He got my attention and asked, "Doesn't your father work here?"

I told him, "Yes."

He told me to stay by the door and start shining shoes. Within minutes, I had my first customer. After a while, I noticed the other shoe-shine men were doing some fancy moves with their shoe-shine brushes.

It was rough with all the competition all around me. I had to do something myself. So I would throw my shoe-shine brush in the air and catch it as I was shining the customers' shoes, and sometimes, I made an extra five-cent tip. I had a few customers, and I managed to rake in about thirty-five cents, so I called it a day. I told the doorman thanks, and that I'd see him again really soon.

I was not used to shining shoes with someone's foot in them. The hardest task was when a customer was wearing white socks; I would sometimes get shoe polish on them no matter how careful I was. Then, I would hope they didn't see it until they paid me. If they wore dark socks, I was safe.

There were some days I could not stay too long because I knew my mother would be wondering where I was. I had to pace myself when I was working and get home before she missed me. I had to be careful because my sisters, many times, would watch me like a hawk, and they were getting somewhat suspicious.

Between my homework and Greek school, I had a hard time trying to shine shoes during the week. So I had to concentrate on the weekends.

Then I found out my buddy the doorman was off on weekends. I knew that was going to create a problem. Sure enough, when I went to the hotel entrance, the other doorman chased me. I tried to explain to him that the other doorman would allow me to stay by the door.

He did not care and said, "Get lost!" So between the other shoe guys and the doorman, I had a hard time trying to make any money. Location was everything. I had no choice, so again I went home without making a nickel.

That Monday after school, I ran over to the hotel and saw my friend. I explained to him what had happened with the other doorman. He assured me he would talk to him about it. Then he said, "Go to work." Within minutes, I had a customer; I was on a roll. Everything was working in my favor.

One day, this beautiful, well-dressed woman, who looked like a model or perhaps an actress, wanted her shoes shined. She was so pretty I could not take my eyes off her. I shined her shoes, which did not take long even though I took my time. When I finished, I said, "That will be five cents."

She opened up her purse, handed me a five-dollar bill, and said, "Keep the change." I was so excited, I was speechless. I could not thank her enough.

The doorman asked me, "Do you know who that woman was? Her name is Dorothy Lamour. She is a famous actress."

All I knew was she was remarkably pretty.

With everyone getting somewhat suspicious, I decided to take a short time off. I figured I had made enough money to keep me for a while.

The doorman must have spoken with my father when he did not see me for a while. Dad came down on me about it and said I was out of the shoe-shine business. He explained I was too young to be working; I had my whole life in front of me.

I said to myself, "That was a short business encounter"; even though I only worked a short time, that extra money felt terrific.

I came to find out then that the average family income was anywhere from twenty-three to thirty-five dollars a week or thirty-five to forty cents an hour. The cost of a loaf of bread was about fourteen cents a loaf, and if one could afford to own a car, which averaged about $900 to $1200 dollars, gas was about nineteen cents a gallon. A stamp to mail a letter was three cents. A house cost anywhere from five to ten thousand dollars.

Dad would, on occasion, bring home this massive can of peanuts from work. Mom had to hide them, because we would eat them as if there were no tomorrow. Mom would later ration them out when we behaved.

During the school week, after supper, we did homework, and then we would gather around the radio. We fought for the front seat. One would think it was a movie the way we argued about it.

We would listen to shows like *The Squeaking Door, The Shadow Knows, Racket Squad, Captain Video, The Lone Ranger, Superman, The Green Hornet, The Jack Benny Show, The Life of Riley, Boston Blackie, Our Miss. Brooks, Amos and Andy, The Answer Man, Philip Morris Playhouse, The Whistler* and many others. Those were the good old days!

On Sundays, we all looked forward to going to the picture show movie after church services. After we had lunch, we would get twenty-five cents for the movie and a snack. We all went together; sometimes we would meet some friends at the movie theater.

Our favorite movie theater was Lowe's on Fifty-First Street and Lexington Avenue. We sometimes went to the RKO near Bloomingdale's on Third Avenue. No matter what theater we went to, we would always see a cartoon, a newsreel, coming attractions, and not one, but two feature movies.

Before going to the seats, we would buy snacks. My favorites were Good & Plenty, Mary Jane's, Milk Duds, and Almond Joys. Sometimes, I bought things like wax Coke-bottle shapes with colored sugar water, Black Jack chewing gum, and these candy dots that were on this long piece of white paper.

When it was time to leave, we would try to stay longer by sneaking into the balcony. No matter what we did, the ushers always caught us and sent us home.

My friends and I would go to the Saturday matinee downtown on Fourteenth Street and see different movies starring Gene Autry, Roy Rogers, and Dale Evans. We also watched Tarzan and all those science-fiction thrillers.

Now that I think back, the only sex on screen was a girl in a bathing suit. Movie stars even kissed with their mouths closed—at least they did in the movies. When it came to violence, it was two people shooting it out. The only bad habit was many actors would smoke.

There were no movie ratings because all the movies that we saw were responsibly produced for all to enjoy, without violence or profanity or most anything offensive. Everything was left to the imagination. Boy, how times have changed!

A new concept came to the movie theaters in the early fifties; it was called three-dimension, better known as 3-D. In order to see this effect, one had to wear these particular eyeglasses. Then 3-D comic books came out soon thereafter.

I remember when the fruit and vegetable man would come to the neighborhood to sell his produce; he was on a horse-drawn wagon. For a dollar, Mom was able to buy so many fresh fruits and vegetables.

Sometimes, when he sold out, some of us would take a ride with him. He would take his horse and wagon to the stables down on Twenty-Third Street. I never told my mother, because she would never have let me go. I just had to sneak to make sure that she never saw me.

It was fun riding on the horse-drawn wagon as we were going down Second Avenue. The only drawback was as the horse was moving so was his digestive system. I had to hold my nose most of the time. When we got to the stable, he would remove the horse from the harness, and the horse would gallop right to his stall. I would help him get the wagon ready for the next day.

Living in the same neighborhood, we would go home together. I always looked forward to going home on the Third Avenue el. He would many times give me ten cents or sometimes an apple or two for helping him.

Just like with everything else, I would take notice and see how things were changing as I was growing up. It was not much longer before his business, and many other small businesses like the iceman's, went the same way as the horse and buggy did.

During the summer, this large truck would come to the neighborhood and park right in front of the apartment house and sell these immense watermelons for fifty cents each. I never enjoyed eating them because of the black pits. I would say, "Why can't they make them pitless?" It reminds me of that old saying that if one wishes enough, sometimes the wish comes true.

We would always listen for the Good Humor man, who would come on his tricycle with his bells ringing. We would all line up like soldiers to buy our favorite types of ice cream. Again, if we did not behave, guess who was not getting ice cream. It seemed when he came, we all had on our halos. Other times, we would wait for the knish man; for just five cents, it was a treat we all looked forward to.

Sometimes, a few of us would chip in a few pennies and buy a bottle of soda pop. We would then choose (by way of "Eeny-meeny-miney-mo") who got that first sip, and then the next guy would wipe the bottle with his shirt. Then on days when we had no money, we would drink from the water hose when the grocer was washing down the sidewalk; it was unbelievable that no one ever got sick.

One of my friends had this Sears catalog, and I would go through the toy pages and drool. I would dream of owning some of them.

I was always interested when things were changing. For example, there was a time when all the avenues went both ways and then they made them one way. It seemed funny at first seeing vehicles only going in one direction. I noticed it took a while for drivers to get into the new traffic pattern. For a while, I would watch from the window, like I was watching a movie, all the head-on accidents and near misses.

I learned the reason why it was done; it was so traffic would move a lot more easily and to reduce the number of head-on collisions.

I also remember when all the traffic lights were just red and green. That was a moment to see with all the accidents. It was a smart thing somebody woke up and brought the yellow light into the picture.

The only main streets they left two ways were the eight major cross streets in the center of Manhattan. Starting with Fourteenth Street, Twenty-Third Street, Thirty-Fourth Street, Forty-Second Street, Fifty-Seventh Street, Eighty-Sixth Street, Ninety-Six Street, and 125th Street. There were other two-way streets downtown, like Canal Street and Houston Street (pronounced "How-Ston").

I also realized the traffic flow on the cross streets ran a certain direction. The even numbered would go west to east, and the odd numbered would go east to west, but there were a few exceptions.

Many times, before supper, Harry and I would play a game we called "counting the cars." We would pick a color and whichever color of car there was the most of during a light change would win. That was when cars were basic colors!

I used to hate when it rained, because there was not much to do but hang out in the apartment. One afternoon, I got bored, so I got dressed up in my raincoat and galoshes and decided to make the most of it. Mom asked why I was going out on this terrible day. I just said, "I want to go out."

She said, in her usual manner, "Be careful and do not get lost."

It was raining pretty hard; I saw things flowing in the gutter and had a terrific idea. I ran back upstairs to ask Dad to teach me how to make a paper boat. He laughed. He said, "Now, I'm getting ready to leave for work."

Mom said, "Leave your father alone; I will make it."

After Dad had left for work, Mom showed me how to make a paper boat. She asked why all of a sudden I was so interested in paper boats. After she had made one, I ran downstairs to try the boat out. I took the paper boat and put it in the moving water, and it just took off. I chased it, but before I was able to grab it, it went into the storm drain.

I tried to make one myself. Mom asked what had happened to the one she had made. I told her it went down the sewer. She laughed and said that I could not use paper, because it would only fall apart. I said, "I know," but it cost nothing to make.

Once my friends saw what I was doing, we would have races. Rainy days were not that boring anymore.

The cap gun was a big thing, but owning one was something many of us did not have the satisfaction of at the beginning. We would buy the caps for pennies, and to fire them off, we used a small rock. Sometimes, we would throw the caps into a fire, where they would make a thunder sound..

When I was young, we started going to Staten Island for most of the summer. We would take the Staten Island ferry, and then we took the train. I remember the town New Dorp. Dad would rent out a bungalow, which was within walking distance of the beach.

This was the family getaway from the city hassle. Dad would come on weekends when he was off or on vacation. A lot of my cousins also spent the summer there. I made a lot of friends, some of whom lived there year-round, and others, just like us, who came for the summer.

Some of the local guys would play tricks on us city guys. I remember them telling us that there was a haunted house with ghost. I was just beginning to love scary things like that, so I welcomed the challenge of exploring this haunted house. The problem was nobody ever wanted to go with me.

Every year, whenever we went for the summer, I would always talk about the haunted house. Every time I would bring it up, the others would change the subject.

Since I was from the city, fishing was something I'd never done before we went there. Whenever we went to the beach, I would see the older guys fishing. They had a small rowboat, and they would go far out into the bay. I remember one of the guys was named Richard. I think my sister Tessie had a crush on him.

So if I wanted to try fishing, I would have to go on my own. I would fish from the rocks. Mom never liked it and would scold me whenever I went anywhere near the rocks.

One Saturday, Richard and some of his friends never came back from their fishing trip. For hours, they searched for them with no luck. When Mom heard about this, she became more cautious with us. She would keep a sharper eye on us when we went to the beach. So that ended my short fishing career.

I kept some fishing hooks that I still had hidden back home. For the longest time, nobody ever found them, until one day, my brother Jack was reaching for something where I had them hidden and he managed to hook one of his fingers. He gave out with a scream, and Mom ran to see what had happened. She gave me such a beating I do not know which hurt more, Jack's finger or my rear.

When Dad came for the weekend, he would tell us the latest news. He told us that a US B-25 military airplane had crashed into the Empire State Building during a fog. The crash killed all three crew members and some office workers and injured many more. He also heard that an elevator operator survived a seventy-five-floor plunge. Tell me God was not watching out for that individual! He told us from the apartment house, it looked as if the sky was on fire.

I also remember we did not go one summer because of a serious fire that destroyed the terminal in Staten Island.

Dad would always bring us the newspapers while we were away. I read an article in the newspaper about a flying saucer that allegedly crashed somehow in Roswell, New Mexico, in July of 1947. There was testimony about what people saw; some even claimed they saw dead creature-like bodies, but the government later dismissed it. They claimed it was a weather balloon.

I always wonder because the government said that we had to believe what they reported. There was talk about a possible cover-up.

As I was growing up, I believed less in the government. I started to believe that they never told the public the real truth about many things.

I also read that the first African-American baseball player was going to play in the majors. His named was Jackie Robinson; he started playing in the 1947 season for the Brooklyn Dodgers. There was a lot of consistent catcalls on the field, as well as off the field.

I could not believe the hostility that so many people carried. Was I too naive to understand? It was something I realized would not disappear. Thank God that there is more love, and that seems to drown out some of the hate.

Many times, I would go shopping with my mother. After she got the grocery items, we would go to another store for the meat. We went to this chicken farm to get a live chicken. Mom would pick out a chicken from a whole flock.

I was speechless when I saw the man take the chicken and cut off its head with an ax. Then he plucked off its feathers with this machine and wrapped it in this butcher paper. I somehow lost my appetite.

When we bought chicken from the regular butcher, I never gave it much thought, but after seeing this, I had a different outlook when I ate chicken.

Vacation was just about winding down, that meant school was just around the corner. Summer always seemed to fly by, yet winter seemed to last forever.

When the weather was still warm, we would go to a city park that was within walking distance from where we lived. It had swings and slides, plus other fun things that we certainly looked forward to.

One day, I saw some boys, who were a little older, doing something that got my attention. They were sliding down the slide; they would jump off it halfway down. The next time I was on the slide, being a typical boy, I decided to try the same.

Oops! I guess my timing was off. It seems my earlobe got caught on the corner on the handle, and I tore my earlobe. There was blood all over me. The next thing I knew, they were taping up my ear in the hospital. Now that taught me a kindly lesson not to do everything I saw, just because someone else did it. Mom would always say, "Wait until you are parents."

In 1948, Mom and Dad were terribly upset when they heard a rumor that President Truman had lost to Governor Dewey. The good news was some of the news media had the facts wrong, which only proves you cannot believe everything you read.

Dad was constantly going in and out of the hospital for different kinds of tests. His health was not getting any better. Then it happened; one day, he never came home. I did not know what to expect.

I remember my brothers and my mother talking to a gentleman. Then when he left, Mom gave him some of Dad's clothing. Little did I know, it was for his funeral viewing.

From that time on, I realized I would never be walking to work with Dad and our chats would only be a memory. I could not get over all the people at his viewing. It is amazing that it takes times like this to see relatives and friends.

Things were not the same for a long, long time. Mom had been left with five children, from six to sixteen years old, to raise.

I was extremely bitter when Dad died. I was thinking to myself, *Why our*

Dad? He was a pleasant and loving father. In my eyes, he passed away much too young. At that time, a man's life expectancy was mid-sixties.

They say time heals all wounds, but when it is someone really close, it feels like forever. It was customary to wear black for a full year after a member of the family passed. Mom took it a lot longer.

Mom had no choice but to go on welfare, as much as she did not want to. I could sense it was going to be extremely difficult and a financial hardship to try to make ends meet with five children.

My brothers got jobs while they were still going to school. My brother Harry quit high school when he was sixteen years old. He always put family first and got a full-time job to help. He then went to night school to finish school and graduated. I would tease him because the school was an all-girl school during the day classes.

Harry was extremely close to Mom. He would do most anything to help and please her. I was now seeing Harry in a different light and saw him as more than just a brother.

Like I said, Mom was not keen on hospitals. Now that Dad had passed away in one, she was certainly never entering one, much less going for her surgery. She lived with her problem and would buy a new support garment whenever she felt the old one was no longer doing the job.

I was just about to turn ten years old when this all happened. I felt the need to get a job, but nobody would hire me at my age. I continued to go to different merchants in the neighborhood. All I got was the response that I was too young. I thought about shining shoes again, but I remembered what my father had told me, so I respected his wishes.

Mom would go to the cemetery religiously, especially when it was a holiday. We would go with her many times while we were growing up. She would take the *Thimiata* ("holy senses") to the cemetery and bless Dad's grave.

I will always remember the remark she would make, "When I am in the ground with your father, will you still come to the cemetery?"

When we took the bus on First Avenue to church, we always passed this construction site where they were building the United Nations plaza. My friends and I would sneakily check it out after it opened in 1950. It was on seventeen acres of land overlooking the East River. This area was known as Turtle Bay; the name goes back to 1639 and was given by the colonial governor of New Amsterdam.

As usual, we were curious to see what was inside. We sneaked into the back of the general assembly building. It was not too long before the security guards spotted us and chased us out. Over the years, I was still curious and would go sometimes on my own to learn more about it, but through the front doors.

I also came to discover they had their own security police and fire department. They even had their own post office. The only problem was one could only send letters or postcards from their complex if one used their stamps. Visitors from all over the world would mail postcards with United Nations' stamps.

We eventually got a telephone and a black-and-white TV. At that time, people were not permitted to have these nonessentials when they were on welfare; we had to keep a sharp eye out.

I remember when the social workers came unannounced, we all ran around like chickens, trying to hide the TV in the bedroom on the bed and put blankets over it. Then to top it off, there were times we forgot to mute the phone.

It was unbelievable what Mom had to go through with all these different obstacles in order to raise a family. Years later, they started to get more up-to-date as to what essentials were permitted.

Another step toward progress—first the refrigerator, then the washer and dryer, and now the phone and television—what will be next? Now that we had new things like a television, we had something new to argue over.

We all got hooked on watching television and loved to watch many shows, like *I Love Lucy*, which debuted in 1951, and *The Jackie Gleason Show* and *The Liberace Show* in 1952, which came on the air in 1952, and The Life of Riley. The classic family programs were *Father Knows Best, Leave It to Beaver,* and *Ozzie and Harriet.* There were other shows like *The Colgate Comedy Hour with Martin and Louis, Your Show of Shows,* and *Arthur Godfrey* (the redhead).

Mom had her favorite shows like *The Ed Sullivan Show,* which first started in 1948 and ran until 1971, and game shows like *The Price Is Right, Truth or Consequences,* and *Let's Make a Deal.* No one dared to switch channels when she was watching her shows.

Mom even got hooked on watching wrestling. She would get so involved with the wrestling matches she would start screaming at the television. As we were growing up, wrestling was one highlight that we all hated. There were times we would skip over that channel to make her think it was not airing. It did not take her long to catch on that we were trying to deceive her. With only one television, we had to vote which programs we were going to watch.

My sisters loved watching the *Mickey Mouse Show* with the Mouseketeers. My brothers would always change the channel. I could take it or leave it. My favorite shows were shows like *Captain Video* or *Superman.*

During the Christmas holidays, we all enjoyed watching the Christmas specials like Perry Como's and Andy Williams'. It was a time of year that brought us even closer as a family.

We had a limited number of stations to watch: channels 2 to 13. The reception was always terrible, and with all the tall buildings around us, it made for all these shadows on the screen. At first, all we had was what we called "rabbit ears" for the antenna.

My brother Jack was always experimenting; he would put a long wire on the antenna hoping to get better reception. Then he would have me walk the hallway almost to the door just to try to get a fairly decent picture. We eventually got a roof antenna, which was slightly better.

At midnight, they would play the national anthem, recite a poem about God, and all the stations would sign off until 6:00 a.m. the next morning. If you suffered from insomnia in those days you were out of luck.

From watching television, I got hooked on these commercial offers. I remember asking Mom to buy a product called Ovaltine. I needed the label to purchase this Captain Video helmet. She did but got upset, because I never drank it. Mom would call the shows I watched *"sockamotters"* (nonsense.)

When we first got the telephone, we had to share the phone line. They called it a party line. My mother would yell at me because I used to listen to other people's phone conversations. Was that wrong? Now they call it "phone tapping"!

When summer rolled around, we were on the go. Mom started sending us to the church camp called Camp Olympia. The director of the camp was a friend of the family, so between that and the church, the cost to Mom was minimal.

We took a charter bus called Trailway and the bus ride seemed to last forever. The camp was in the far corner of New Jersey near a town called Branchville. We only went for a few weeks. At first, I could not get used to it. The first year, I got homesick. At the beginning, we even talked about sneaking out of camp and going home. As the years passed, we got more into enjoying it.

I remember Mr. Nick, the director, teasing me and telling me about a new food product called "Bird Eyes." I was thinking to myself, *What the heck is that?* Then I found out it was a new frozen-food company named Birds Eye Frozen Foods. These products were a new feature in the grocery-store freezer. Frozen foods became a whopping success back in the early fifties since by then most all had a freezer in their refrigerator.

Mom would come to visit us with my godmother. They would spend a few hours, and then when they left, we all felt homesick. I think it gave Mom a break in a way not to have to cook or wash clothes for all of us.

Mr. Nick had an old ambulance, which he had gotten from the World

War II surplus and converted into a passenger vehicle. He even gave it a name; he called it "Buffo" (not reliable). He would use it to transport some of us back and forth when we went on different field trips. I remember a few times, it would stall out. Sometimes we all would push it. Other times, we all had to get out and walk because it could not make a steep hill. So we all knew the reason he gave it that name.

We would go on many different types of day trips, and many times we went roller-skating, which I loved. We would play games while we were skating. We would make a loop, and then we would skate as fast as we could go. The others would let go of my hand, and then I would go crashing into the guardrails and sometimes the wall. It was surprising how I never got hurt.

Many of the older guys would go skinny-dipping in this out-of-the-way brook. I was too small, so they never let me go. I remember my brother Harry and a few others sat on some poison ivy once. Must I say anything else?

We all started getting to enjoy going to camp, and then years later, Mother Nature hit us in 1954 with Hurricane Hazel. It did a lot of damage. The following year, another hurricane, Connie, totally destroyed the campgrounds. What was the likelihood that it could happen twice, in the same location? So that ended the summer getaway at Camp Olympia.

One thing I will say about our mother, she was forever cleaning or cooking. Where she got all her energy from, only God knows. Mom would iron all the clothes, including the underwear. She would keep a glass of water next to her, so she could dampen the clothes, as she needed. When I saw this, I came up with an idea. I wanted to make things easier for her when she would iron.

I made her a sprinkle bottle from an empty Coke bottle. I made small holes in the cap, so when she needed to wet any item she was ironing, she now had the convenience of sprinkling her clothes instead of getting them too wet. Steam irons were unheard of. She would say "Maestro Mecheles" (Mike the engineer).

Mom had this Singer sewing machine she had to turn by hand. Many times, she would ask one of us to thread the needle. We would tease her, and she would simply say, "Just wait till you get to my age."

Mom was a fabulous cook; everybody praised her cooking and baking, including me, even if there were meals she made that I did not eat. The pots and pans she used for cooking looked old even then, but I think there was magic in them.

Mom sometimes would bake even though it was not a holiday. She would make the "*koulourakia*" (butter cookies), and of course, she would hide them from us. Again, she would bake while we were in school. Even though she cleaned up the evidence, we could smell the aroma the baking left.

My brothers gave me the responsibility for locating her hiding place. One Saturday, when everybody was out, I went searching for it, and I found the "*koulourakia*". I found them hidden among some linen she had in her dresser drawer.

I grabbed one, bit into it, and spit it out. I could not believe how awful the taste was. It was so bland. I told Harry about them. He said, "You're crazy. Let me try one." Sure enough, he agreed, they were terrible. What were we to do? If we told her, she would know that I'd been looking for them. One of us had to tell her, and guess who it was.

I remember telling her, "Do not get mad at me, but I found the "*koulourakia*". I tried them. They're awful."

She started yelling at me. Then she tried one herself and shouted, "I forgot the sugar!" The real shame was she had made a double batch. Mom was so upset she was almost in tears. We all felt terrible because just to make a single batch was a job in itself.

Mom started mumbling, "That damn telephone." It seems she had answered the phone while she was baking and forgot the sugar. From that day on, whenever she baked, the phone was off-limits. And when she baked, I was also her personnel food taster. I guess sometimes telling does have its rewards.

Mom was extremely strict when we were young when it came to outside activities. For example, on Halloween, we had to stay together. We also did not have the luxury of going to the store to buy a costume.

We had to be creative and make our own costumes if we wanted to go trick-or-treating. There was this one Halloween Mom had me dress like a raggedly old woman; all my friends teased me. After trick-or-treating, we had to hide some of the candy. Mom would limit what we could eat.

Chapter 4

A Learning Experience

We all attended the same grammar school, P.S. 116, as we were growing up. My brothers and I had to wear a white shirt and a tie to school, with no exceptions. We would walk to school, which was about seven long blocks away. When the weather was nice, the walk was not that awful, but when it was cold or raining, it seemed like miles. I was always wearing out my shoes, as were my brothers and sisters, by putting holes in the soles.

We had a shoemaker just downstairs, and if we were lucky, we would have them repaired, but that was rare. Mom could not afford to buy us new shoes or even repair them very often.

We had to take other measures, like putting cardboard in the shoes until we got new ones. There were times we had to fight over the cardboard from the cereal box tops, so we could resole them.

Every Tuesday was bank day. Mom would give us a dime to put into the school savings account. I can still remember the bank's name: the Bowery Savings Bank. We also got a few pennies to buy war bonds stamps.

Years later, I thought about putting some of my earnings and tip money in the account. The problem arose when I needed some money; I came to find out getting it out was not as easy as depositing it. To make withdrawals from the account, a parent's signature was required. That took care of that idea, and I just kept that money well hidden.

Mom would make lunch every day for all of us. She would brown bag it, and I could always tell my lunch from the other students'. You ask how? My bag was always greasy looking. Mom, many times, would make us an omelet or peanut butter and jelly sandwiches during Lent and every Friday.

Many times, my classmates and I would trade lunches, just so it would not get boring.

Even though pizza came to America in the early 1900s, I discovered pizza for the first time while I was in grammar school. One day during the school lunch period, a few of us went to this Italian grocery store to research something new: pizza pie.

I could not even imagine what it looked like or even tasted like, but I remember it was ten cents a slice. When I first tasted it, I burned the roof of my mouth and some of the cheese slid down my chin, burning it as well. After that first taste, I got hooked.

There were many times we had to practice in school for air-raid drills, in case of a nuclear attack; duck and cover was the thing to do. It was a scary time; many families were talking about building bomb shelters in case of an air attack. We would always talk about what life would be like if ever there was a nuclear attack. I still could not help thinking about it, because all it would take was just one crazy individual to push the button. Was I seeing too many movies or reading too many comic books?

Being boys, my friends and I would be constantly fooling around. It was a Friday afternoon, and silly me, I threw the chalkboard eraser at one of my friends. Well, he ducked, and I hit the teacher while he was writing on the blackboard.

He turned around and asked who was the wise guy. I hesitated at first, and then I got up and apologized. He told me to report to Miss O'Hara's office (the principal) right away and tell her what had happened.

I was a nervous wreck; here it was, almost 3:00 p.m., time to go home, and I had to report to the principal's office. I walked into her office and told her what I did. She scolded me and said, "Monday morning, I want to see you in my office, before going to your class."

This had to be one weekend that I never wanted to see come to an end. My mother could even sense my attitude because I was not myself. Monday morning came, and I slowly walked into her office. I told her I was not intentionally trying to hit the teacher. I apologized for being so stupid, and I promised her I would not be there again.

She asked what I thought was a fair punishment for my inappropriate behavior. I said, "Whatever."

She said, "Okay, for one week, you are to clean the teachers' blackboard erasers after lunch."

I would never tell my mother about my school punishments because I knew she would scold me. It would not end there, because she'd ground me, too. I would try to keep it a secret as long as I could, but sometimes the teacher would send a note home with me, and Mom had to sign it. I tried fudging her signature, but I got caught, so that ended that.

Some of my classmate friends would shout some of the bad Greek words in the classroom. The teacher would always point to me and then scold me for teaching them those words. I tried to deny it; nevertheless, he warned me. If it happened again, guess who was going to the principal's office.

Another time, a fight broke out in the lunchroom, and I got in trouble for just watching and not trying to stop it. The monitor said I had not tried to stop the fight but supported it, so I went to the principal's office for that, which I felt was unfair. The first thing she asked was what I was doing there after I promised I wouldn't be back. I assured her that I would not be sent to her office again. She made me water her plants before going to my classroom every morning for a week.

One of my classmates dared me to put a thumbtack on this one girl's seat. Stupid me, you would think I'd know better. I did it, and soon was back in the principal's office again. I had to apologize to the girl; plus I had to stay after school for one week except for the days I had Greek school. After the week of detention, the principal said, "I do not want to see you in my office again."

One day, a few of us decided to go out for our lunch break. Not realizing we were late, we tried to sneak back. As we were sneaking back in, the monitor caught us, and we got sent to the principal's office. When she saw me, she said I was making a habit of coming to the office. She scolded us and sent the other two back to the classroom.

Then she went on to say, "What am I going to do with you? I cannot remember either of your brothers ever coming to the office the way you have."

I apologized again and said, "I promise I will not be sent to your office again." I must have sounded like a broken record.

A short time later, she saw me in the hallway and said to me, "I want to see you in my office after lunch."

I was thinking to myself, *What the heck did I do now, that she wants to see me?*

As I was walking to her office, I was thinking, *Did I do something I did not remember?*

She said, "Do not get worried. I called you in for another reason."

It was as if something heavy had been lifted off my shoulders. She was seeking volunteers to help set up an affair that the school was holding in the auditorium. What a relief it was to hear that.

Every Friday, we had assembly, and all the classes would attend. Miss. O'Hara would read a passage from the Bible, and afterward, we all sang the

"Star-Spangled Banner." It was so quiet you could hear a pin drop; that was how well behaved everybody was.

After all this, I became particularly helpful to the school principal. Whenever she needed a job or favor, she would call me. There were times I would leave the school grounds to go to the board of education to get some valuable papers; I also went to a restaurant to retrieve her eyeglasses, which she had left behind. My brother Harry had done these same errands just before he went on to another school.

My fellow students and my friends were calling me a gofer and her pet. Let's just say being her so-called pet had its advantages.

One of the students was so bold and stupid, he decided instead of taking a test, he would send a false fire alarm. The school was immediately evacuated, causing many students to panic. Shortly thereafter, when things settled down, everybody returned to the classrooms. The student who made the false alarm was reprimanded, and he still had to take the test, which only proves stupidity gets you nowhere, but in trouble.

Lice were a serious problem and were out of control. Mom, every night, would check our hair using this distinctive comb. Even the schools would check everybody's hair, and if you had any signs of them, you were sent home with no questions asked.

We had many different activities during the school year. I used to hate when we did the square dancing. It seemed I always got stuck with either the largest girl or the not-so-pretty ones.

Now, when we played games like dodgeball, I could never get enough. The one day that stood out was the May Day Festival. It celebrated the coming of spring, which meant the school season was coming to an end.

I always had a fairly hefty appetite, especially if I enjoyed what Mom made for supper. Whenever I got home after school and just before going to do my homework or play, I would enjoy a snack. I would enjoy a bowl of cereal, puffed wheat, or rice, or see my friend at the tavern.

I hated getting haircuts mainly because of all the itching from the falling hair. My favorite haircut was a crew-cut. Summer came, and I would get my hair cut really short. This way, I did not have to go as often.

One day, while we were waiting, I heard Jimmy the barber asking one of the other customers if he knew anyone who wanted a job. When I heard that the job was cleaning up on the weekend, I hung around.

I said, "I would like the job. Let me prove I can do it. If you don't appreciate my work, don't pay me."

He hesitated a second, and then he laughed and said, "Okay."

Now I had to convince Mom, which was no easy task. When I told her, she did not like the idea. She asked, "Do I know this Jimmy?" I told her he was the barber. She paused, but because it was only on weekends and nearby, she said, "Okay."

I started that weekend. It was only Friday and Saturday after he closed for two hours, and I got paid twenty-five cents a day. Plus, he gave me free haircuts; even Mom liked that.

The job was fun. He had this barber's pole that I would wind up to get the red and blue strips to spin. The only part I did not enjoy was that I had to clean the spittoon. After the first weekend, he said the job was mine.

I would also run errands for the men who hung out in a local *Kafenion* (men's coffee hangout) where they would play cards, smoke, eat, and drink. Now between my weekend job and this, I was earning an average of a buck and sometimes more. I gave my mother most of the money. I would keep about twenty-five cents for myself until I got paid again.

My brothers and I would laugh because on Saturday nights, it got to be a habit at the Kafenion, the police would come with the paddy wagon and take them all away because they were gambling. The funny part was no sooner than they were back from jail they were back playing cards again as if nothing had happened.

Most of my friends had a bicycle or were getting one, and I wanted one myself. I knew my mother could not afford to buy me one. In order to buy my bike, I had to start saving some money. I told Mom I had decided to save all my money. She asked, "For what?"

I told her it was a surprise.

I also started doing deliveries for a local repair shop called Irving's Fix It Shop. The owner taught me about electricity and how to repair different small appliances. I owe most of my knowledge of electricity to his expertise.

As we were growing up, electricity was DC, direct current. Then it was converted to what we know today as AC, alternating current. Many times, we would blow a fuse, because of an overload, so we had to go to the cellar to replace it. Some people would put a metal slug instead of the round fuses to avoid replacing it. The drawback was that many buildings caught fire, and some burned down because of stupidity.

One of my friends, who also worked at the fix-it shop, wanted to pull a trick on me. We were always playing jokes on each other. He wanted to give me an electrical shock, but the joke was on him. It seems that he was holding these two wires that came out of this control panel looking to shock me when he accidentally touched the wire and shocked himself. The bad part was because it was DC electricity, it was holding him, and he could not let go until the power was off. The owner, Irving, turned off the power. My friend was still shaking even after the power was off. He and I both learned a new lesson that day: electricity is your slave unless it gets ahold of you, so respect it.

A few of my friends loved to gamble. They would toss dimes against a wall; the one who got it closest to the wall would win the pot. Sometimes, one could make fifty cents on just one round.

The more that played, the bigger the pot, so they asked me to play. Since I was saving for my bike, I figured maybe I could make money the easy way. Big mistake. The first time I played, within ten minutes, I had lost almost a dollar.

Maybe I was being too conservative, because I worked too hard to lose money that fast. Somehow, my mother found out. I wonder who spilled the beans. Mom said, "That is what one gets when one gambles." Another lesson I learned: if you want something that awfully, earn it.

My friends and I always wanted to start a club, but we could never find a decent location. So we agreed that I should ask Jimmy about using the basement. I waited to ask him when he was in a giving way. When I did ask, he said a flat "No way."

I told the gang, "No luck." We were all somewhat disappointed with his answer.

A short time later, he said to me it was okay to use the basement. Then he explained I had to be responsible for any problems that might occur. So I assured him he need not worry; I would take full responsibility. I told my friends about the circumstances and that I was going to take charge. The only drawback was we could only use it during store hours when he was open, with no exceptions. I told the gang it was better than having nothing.

When I explained all the details, all of my friends, except one, were pleased and agreed with the terms. He did not agree because he felt that because he was older, he should be in charge. I said, "Okay, let's vote, and the majority will win." After we all had voted, I won by most of the vote. I made it abundantly clear if he did not agree, he should leave. He eventually changed his feeling and joined the rest of us.

The basement needed a lot of work, so we all pitched in to get it done. We would get things that people were throwing out. When we got done, it looked just like a clubhouse. We would argue over stupid things, and we would call each other names like, "rat fink" and "your mother's uncle."

We all had different ideas on building things. So we put some ideas together to design a go-cart. For example, we got wheels from some old baby carriage and wood, nails, and other miscellaneous items from the janitor's basement. In fact, my friend Louis designed a steering wheel that worked just like a car's.

Between school, homework, and working, it took a while to get it completed. When we finally completed it, we had constructed a go-cart like nobody had ever seen.

We were all so excited about building it, no one ever thought about making measurements. When we were ready to take it out of the basement, we realized it did not fit through the doorway. No matter which means we tried, it just would not fit.

We only had one option: take it apart and reassemble it. Now the problem was we just could not take it apart every time we were going to use it. Right then, we were not going to worry about it, just enjoy it.

Fortunately, we lived near a hill. The top of the hill was called Tudor City, so what better spot to try it? We would take turns riding down the hill. The problem was the bottom of the hill was a main thoroughfare (Second Avenue), and someone had to watch the traffic flow. So we all took turns watching the traffic.

We had it all figured out; when the light turned red, stopping the traffic, we would push the go-cart down the hill. We were all taking turns, and finally it was my turn to go. I pushed the go-cart up the hill and waited for the okay. When I got the motion to go, I pushed it, jumped in, and took off.

I was picking up speed and nearing the bottom of the hill, when my friends shouted, "Jump out!" There was a truck coming. Without thinking twice, I jumped out, and seconds later, the truck hit the cart and smashed it into pieces. I had a few abrasions and cuts.

I yelled out, "Who was the rat fink who gave me the green light to go?" Well, of course nobody would admit it. I had a suspicion who it was, but I was not going to make a vital issue of it. As we were picking up the pieces, we realized the problem of where were we going to keep the go-cart had been solved.

Somehow, my mother found out about the incident; she was all over me. She yelled at me for doing such a stupid thing. She even scolded my friends for it, too. I must have heard this for weeks. Her favorite comment was "Wait till you are parents."

We were all on tight budgets, so anything we needed, we had to make ourselves. It was unbelievable the things we made from scratch. We would make different items, like kites, slingshots, peashooters, and wooden guns. If we could not make it, we had to visit the local F. W. Woolworth's 5 & 10-Cent store on Forty-Second Street and Third Avenue and collect what we needed.

Most of the time, we would luck out and get away with it. Just like everything in life, luck goes just so far. I had it down to a science; when the weather was cold, I would wear this overcoat, which had deep pockets. While I was putting a small, plastic fire engine in my coat pocket, a security guard caught me in the act. All my friends took off like scared cats. He took me to the office where he threatened to call the police and put me in jail.

I had to think fast, make up a heartbreaking story, and just hope it would work. I told him I knew what I did was wrong, but my mother could not afford it. He scolded me and told me if I did it again, I was going to jail. "Tell your friends what I said," he added. When I heard that, I found my halo, and so did most of my friends.

Almost everybody had roller skates. I took some of my savings to buy a pair. The problem was many times, I would lose my skate key. So I attached the key to a string around my neck and kept it secured.

Once in a while, I would have one of the neighbor dogs drag me while I was on my roller skates. Mom never liked it and would yell at me when I did that.

Roller skating was fun, but after a while, it started getting boring. So we all decided to build individual skate carts. All we needed was one roller skate, which we separated into halves; a two-by-four piece of wood about four feet long; and a sturdy wooden milk box, which we got from the local grocer; and a few nails.

The best was when it was assembled. You could not ask for anything better. We would paint numbers on the wooden boxes, and then we would race each other. They took a lot of abuse, because we would beat the heck out of them. The biggest expense was the roller skates, because we would wear them out. Someone was always missing his or her one roller skate—mostly her.

My brother Jack loved to build model planes and other woodcrafts. The biggest thrill was he started to collect Lionel trains; he would buy a piece or two every few weeks until he had a full line of different train cars and accessories. Then he would make a complete layout of tracks and put it on a four-by-eight board. The problem was we were tight on space, but Jack was always coming up with ideas. He would design it where he could raise it up and down from the ceiling when he wanted to run them.

Mom was not too thrilled with his train layout, but he had a way about him that she always gave into him. Nobody could play with the trains unless he was there. I loved trains, but from that time on, I became a real train fanatic.

Jack was extremely creative and would make and build different projects. He had this soldering iron that he used, and the only way he could heat it up was by putting it over the flame on the stove. Mom would shout, "Do not use the stove for that reason!" So to keep peace, he would do it when she was out.

Jack had expensive tastes and always bought the best of anything. He always did things in a unique fashion. He would do things like rent out a movie projector and different movies from a store called Peerless on weekends. We would watch movies; it was almost like being in a real movie theater. He would also rent these World War II movie documentaries, like *Victory at Sea*, which I enjoyed.

Jack bought this expensive brand-name beautiful, hi-fi consol. It looked like a piece of furniture and replaced the old radio.

He would purchase all these different types of LP albums—78, 33, and 45 rpm—and collect them. Come payday, he would buy one or even two every week until he had a large selection. I was always interested to see and learn how music came off this round disc called a "record." Jack told me in the years to come, they would have dozens and possibly even more songs coming off a small disc.

He never liked anyone touching his new records, but especially the hi-fi unless he was there. So because he would yell at me, I would play his records when he was not home. He was a fanatic when it came to his music collection. So to keep them safe, he would carefully store all his records, and the 45 records he kept in this long rack which he would be constantly dusting off.

While Mom was cleaning, she moved them and by accident put them on the top of the steam radiator. Jack was not too thrilled about his wavy 45 record collection.

My brother Harry was quite a guy. I always looked up to him. He was only a few years older, but more than that, he was always my hero. He was also "big" for his age, and because of that, he looked older. He would watch over us; he was like a father figure. I was on the short side for my age, and I would occasionally get picked on.

I remember two older and bigger guys calling me nasty names. They also tossed my hat into the street where there was water. My brother Harry saw this and came to my rescue. There were other times I was not quite as lucky, and I had to take my licks or fight back.

My brothers would always be horsing around when they were home alone. One day, they were fooling around and somehow they managed to break the glass on the interior door. They cleaned up the mess and hoped nobody would notice it; that was wishful thinking. I knew nothing about what had occurred, but somehow, I got blamed. When Mom saw the glass was missing, they told her, "Mikey did it." Though I told her I did not do it, I still got blamed.

After our father had passed away, we had a lot of visitors, and some were even from out of town. It was always fun to have company, because Mom was a little more flexible, and we would take advantage of it.

Mom would make different types of Greek dishes, like "*Locanica*" (Greek sausage), especially when we had visitors. And she would cook it over an open flame on top of the gas stove. She would also make these different dips, like "*Taramosalata*" (fish roe salad) and "*Tzatziks*" (cucumbers and garlic). These were some of the appetizing Greek foods I would never eat, even if I was hungry.

Now, when Mom made things like "stuffed peppers", *"Dolmathes"* (stuffed grape leaves), or *"Keftethes"* (fried meatballs) that was a different story; we always looked forward to eating the extra fillings. When she made things like chocolate pudding, we all would fight over the leftovers. Mom would yell at us because we always left a mess.

Every Friday, Mom would make fish. My favorite was her Greek-style *"sheputers"* (porgies) with onions and olive oil. Jack and I always looked forward to this meal. Harry and my sisters were not too fond of fish. Jack and I would always argue over the largest piece. Because I was little, so was my piece. Many times, when supper was ready and he was not ready to eat, guess who grabbed and ate the bigger piece.

Mom, every so often, made this Greek chicken soup (*Avgolemono*) that had this thick form of cream on top. To enjoy its fresh taste, it had to be eaten just as soon as Mom finished making it. It was so tasty that we were always looking for more.

Like I said, we had a lot of company. I also remember we had a cousin who came from Baltimore. He would make his own homemade Greek liquor, called *ouzo*. Most people pack clothes in a suitcase, but not him. He would pack bottles of *ouzo*. He would drink it like it was water, and it even looked like water, but that was where the similarity ended. One day, being extremely curious, I had to try some. When no one was paying attention, I grabbed the glass that had just been poured, and I drank it straight down. I remember tasting this licorice flavor. It went down really smoothly. It was lights out; I fell asleep under the table. Everybody was wondering where I had disappeared to. I think from that day on, I got hooked on ouzo.

Sister Mary was a tremendous pain in the_____. There were times I just wanted to_____ (fill in the blank spaces). I am sure I'm not alone when I say we all had one in the family. As she was growing up, her character stayed the same. She was more bark than bite, but what a bark! I think she could even have started an argument with an angel.

Mary was always getting Mom upset over something stupid, which was singularly typical of her. One day, Mom got so upset she tossed her slipper at her. Mary ducked, and the slipper went flying through the open window.

We were living on a busy intersection, and the slipper must have landed on someone's passing vehicle. Mom wanted me to try to get the slipper. I said, "You must be kidding. It is long gone by now."

When Dad was alive, he had the patience of a saint, except when it came to my sister Mary. There were a few times she had him so wound up he was ready to throw her out the window. Luckily, the window was not open.

Tessie was just the opposite. She was usually easygoing and minded her own business. Her only drawback was she had the Pappas temper, and at times, she would throw things; nobody's perfect!

I would always tease Tessie as we were growing up. Every night before going to bed, she would set her hair by using bobby pins. She used so many that she never had enough, and she had to search for more. She would start tearing the house apart, going through drawers or looking between the sofa cushions or on the floor.

The next day, after she had her hairstyle; she would sometimes complain that she had a headache or felt dizzy. I would tease her by telling her, "I think you left a bobby pin in your head."

Many times, to keep ourselves entertained, we played school. I would play a Greek schoolteacher. I would make a lot of jokes and just act stupid and silly. Mom would yell at me because I turned the kitchen upside down with all the changes to make it look like a schoolroom. We would also play the money game and use the figures like trillion and even zillion. This was just another average day while we were growing up. What scares me is the government is now playing with these same figures.

One Saturday morning, while we were all having breakfast, we heard screaming and then banging on the door. Mom ran to the door. It was a neighbor; he was standing there holding his two-year-old son, Ricky. He was screaming with fear in his voice, saying, "He is not breathing!"

Mom just grabbed the boy by his feet and shook him upside down. All of a sudden, this piece of apple came out of his mouth, and he started crying. Heaven only knows what might have happened if Mom had not responded the way she did.

This was one time everyone wanted to hear a child crying. In my eyes, Mom was a hero, and I have always remembered that.

When we went visiting, I especially enjoyed when we took the train. I would stand by the front window and take in the view. When we took the Flushing subway line, we would come to this section that always had water leaking from the ceiling onto the tracks. In my eyes, that did not seem to be normal.

I would tell my brothers about the water. They would say, "That is to be expected," and not to worry. I would even tell the conductors every chance I got. Everybody seemed to push it aside, and for many years, that same leak continued, but nothing was ever done.

Then it happened, about thirty years later, that section collapsed, sending a large piece of concrete onto the tracks. It hit a section of a subway car causing many injuries. I guess no one listened, and then it was too late.

I always looked forward to seeing our other aunt and uncle who lived on the west side, just within walking distance of Times Square. They just had one daughter named Sylvia, who was about Harry's age.

They owned a small Nedtick's style hot dog stand right near the old Madison Square Garden. Harry would sometimes fill in for our uncle, so he could get a touch of fresh air. I used to love getting behind the counter and trying to wait on customers. Mom would scold me whenever I did. I especially enjoyed eating the hot dogs and drinking the orange juice. I guess it was always in my blood!

Mom was extremely tough on me, and I could only just do so much on my own. As much as I never wanted to go against her wishes, there were times I had to sneak behind her back. I had joined a boys' club, but the unfortunate part was it was far from where I lived. I sometimes had to rely on my brothers to take me, if my friend's parents could not.

It was a rough struggle saving for my bike. The hardest part was keeping it a secret from my mother. I could not tell anybody because I was afraid they would tell on me or maybe let it slip out. Mom felt I was too young to have one, and living in the city sure did not help.

Harry was always getting involved with different projects. He was always getting free gifts from selling items from a punch-a-tab card. His biggest gift was when he got a Red Rider BB rifle.

Mom was not too thrilled about the new gift he'd received. She would constantly yell at him when he would take it out of the apartment. Since we lived on the top floor, he would go to the roof and target practice. If I were lucky, sometimes he would allow me to take a few practice shots. He did this for quite a while, but his luck ran out.

Somebody must have spotted him with the BB rifle and notified the police. I will never forget when the police came. Mom tried to warn him about the police coming. She did not tell him fast enough, and before he knew it, it was too late.

The way they escorted him off to the local police station, one would have thought that he was on the list of the ten most wanted. The police confiscated his BB rifle; then he was given a talking to and then sent home.

The *Daily News* was around the corner from where we lived. They had his picture blasted in the middle section of the newspaper; it must have been a quiet day for news. The heading read, "Show-off Marches Off." The superintendent's daughter was sunbathing at the same time he was target shooting. Harry became a celebrity in his own time.

Harry was quite a guy. He got involved in many activates. He was in the school band and played the oboe. It drove Mom up the wall when he practiced at home. Our cat Jingles would also hide during his practice session.

I took on different types of small jobs so that I could buy my bike. I worked for a short time as an ice-cream soda jerk after school. The price of a soda fountain drink was just five cents; and a double scoop ice cream cone was ten cents. I got to make different types of soda drinks like a Lime Rickey. I got to love this one drink called an egg cream. It had no egg in it, but it had this thick cream foam about two inches from the top.

After drinking it, you had this white foam around your mouth and a taste that was splendiferous. Then I was let go, because I was giving all my friends free ice cream. Was that wrong?

Both my brothers hated to go to the dentist, but the school required that every student had to get a certificate every six months, signed by our parents. Many times, they would sign Mom's name and get away with it. As for me, I went every six months, just like an obedient boy, mainly because I had no other choice.

Well, the day came; I had saved enough money to buy a bike. I decided to go all out. I purchased a French racer. It was lightweight; had variable speeds; was bright, fire-engine red; and had whitewall tires, a genuine headlight, and a rear red light.

It felt fantastic to have my own set of wheels. Thank goodness I was able to keep it in the clubhouse basement. I had to keep it out of my mother's view. It was tough trying to enjoy it without my family finding out about it. The unfortunate part was on Sundays and holidays, I could not enjoy the bike because the barbershop was not open.

As the weather was starting to get warm, I was hoping to ride my bike more often. I would ride my bike down to the Staten Island ferry pier, but I was too nervous to take the ferry across to Staten Island. I would tour the Wall Street area; the Brooklyn Battery Tunnel had just opened a few years earlier in 1950.

I decided to take a chance and on weekends and holidays leave my bike under the stairs where I lived. I purchased a chain lock to secure it for safekeeping. For a few weekends, everything was working out. I was the envy of some of my friends.

Somehow, Mom found out about the bike. As much as I did not want to lie, I told her it was a friend's. I was watching it for him. She said, "Just be careful. Give it back to him as soon as possible." So now I had to be even more cautious.

Monday morning, before going to school, I would take my bike back into the clubhouse basement for safekeeping. I was speechless one day when I saw my bike was not there. Someone had broken the chain lock. I was in distress. I could not tell my family, because I'd never told them about it. I felt like I had lost my best friend.

I went to the police station to report my stolen bike before going to school.

When I got there, the sergeant in charge at the front desk told me I had to bring in a parent. I said to myself, "That is not going to work."

When my brother Jack came home from work, I told him what had happened. He said, "What bike? Does Mom know about it?"

I told him, "No. Please do not tell her."

We both went to report the bike stolen.

Well, the bike was not found until one Saturday about a year later. I saw this kid riding this bike that resembled my stolen bike, but it was a different color. I asked the kid, who was younger than I was, where he got the bike. He told me his father had bought it for him just recently.

I asked, "Might I take a closer look at your bike?"

He asked, "Why?"

As I turned the bike over, I noticed the initials I had made secretly. I also noticed a small patch of the original color: red. I yelled out, "This is my bike, and I want it back." The kid started to cry.

A small crowd started to gather around us. This was the luck I had, because this all happened right in front of my apartment house. One would think my rotten luck ended there, but my mother happened to stick her head out the window and noticed all the commotion. She saw me in the middle of it. She shouted down to me asking what was happening. I replied, "Nothing," but being a mother, she had her doubts. She sent my brother Jack down to see what was happening. He came down, and he asked what was going on. I told him, "Remember my bike? Well, I am sure I found it."

The young kid ran home to tell his mother, and she returned with him. I told her the whole story; she told me that his father had purchased the bike from a young man about my age just a few days ago.

The police were notified, and one would think a bank had been robbed, with all the police cars that came. I told them we reported the bike stolen. They impounded the bike pending an investigation.

A few days later, the police wanted to talk to my mother to explain the story. I told them my mother did not speak English or understand it well. I was thinking to myself, *How do I get around this, especially now, when she knows nothing about the bike?* To make matters worse, I had lied to her about the bike. Now that the police told her everything, it would not be long before she came down on me.

When I heard that the individual who had stolen the bike was a friend, I could not believe it. He lived a few blocks from the rest of us. He went on probation because of this. I felt sorry for him. As hard as I had it, his family was in worse shape.

He apologized for doing this and all the stupid things he'd done in the past. He told me he would do almost anything to make up for what he'd done.

I guess I was a forgiving person because I forgave him. We remained friendly until he moved years later.

Now that Mom knew the whole story, she came down on me. With her Greek temper, she yelled at me, asking with what money I'd bought it. I told her I had saved for it. She yelled again, "So that was what you were doing with all the money!" She gave me a hard time because I never told her the truth, but over time, she mellowed out.

My French racer was like rotten luck from the day I recovered it. I was always getting flat tires, and the gears kept changing by themselves. I kept bringing the bike back to the shop to have it fixed. With the constant repairs, it was costing a lot of money.

The worst thing that happened occurred when I was riding my bike this one day; it had just rained earlier, and the cobblestone was still wet and slick like ice. I was being especially careful and keeping my speed down. Out of nowhere, this car door opened, and because of the wet pavement, I could not stop in time. The bike was stopped by the open door, but I just kept going. I flew over the door and slid on the cobblestone for a few feet before I came to a stop. Thank God his window was down. I was all right, except for some scrapes and bruises.

The man started yelling at me for denting his door. He was not even concerned about my well-being. I was in shock as I was picking up my bike. It looked like a pretzel. I yelled out, "Don't you look before you get out of your car!" He told me to stick around. With my bike bent in half, I could not go anywhere. He called the police to report the incident.

When the police arrived, they asked me a lot of questions. I told them I was okay except for the bike. They made out an accident report, and they asked me if I wanted a ride home. I said, "No, thanks." With my luck, my mother would be at the window. So all I could do now was carry my pretzel-shaped bike home.

When Mom found out what had happened, she said in Greek, "*Ka la nsuepopses*" (You get what you deserve), for keeping my bike a secret and lying. I learned a vital lesson that day. When you lie, you just get deeper into lying, and eventually, the truth comes out.

Trouble must have been in my blood. I was always getting into some form of mischief with the superintendent, Ms. Dunberg. Most of the time, it was for stupid things like ringing the doorbells and running off, playing hide-and-seek in the hallways, riding on the dumbwaiter, and throwing water balloons off the roof. Was that so terrible?

My friend Lou and I found this old intercom and decided to connect it to each other's apartments. The super had a fit because we were using the clothesline that ran across the yard. She told my mother, and of course, she yelled at both of us.

I denied any wrongdoing, but she never bought it. Mom would sometimes even ground me when I got out of hand.

I sometimes did some decent deeds, like helping some of the older neighbors with their grocery packages. I always felt sorry for this one particular woman. She lived alone, and I never saw anybody visiting her. She always wore the same clothing.

She would invite me in, but I was always a little worried about going into her apartment, so I never did. She always wanted to give me a tip, but I never took it. I felt she could not truly afford it.

The janitor was a nosey buddy, so when she did not see her for a while, she got suspicious and called the police to investigate her apartment. When she did not respond, the police broke the door down. Sure enough, she was lying in her bed dead.

This I will always remember: they alleged that they found over sixty thousand dollars in cash stuffed under her mattress. I found out she had no living relatives and the money went to the state. Here, I had felt sorry for her, so one could imagine how I felt.

Living on the top floor had its advantages, but it also had its disadvantages. The superintendent helper, who was named Mike, would collect the trash during the week. On the weekends and holidays, we had to take care of it ourselves.

I never looked forward to doing the trash. That meant five floors down and five floors up. After a while, it got to be a tremendous pain. I came to discover my brothers were tossing the trash from the open window instead of walking all the way down.

When it was my turn, I decided if my brothers could do it, I would try airmail too instead of going down the five flights.

I noticed this one day, the trash can cover was off, so what better time to try? So I took careful aim, and then I let go of the trash bag—bull's eye! It went right into the trash can. Unfortunately, when the cover was on, I had no other choice but to walk down.

Once in a while, I would not get a direct hit. It would hit the edge of the trash can, and then the trash bag would explode and the trash would be all over everything. I felt guilty because the janitor had to clean it up. This went on for quite a while. Most of the time, I had direct hits. Then it happened. I guess I had pushed my luck.

I was doing my usual trash airmail drop. I took careful aim and let go. Just as it was going into the trash can, Mike, the janitor, all dressed in his Sunday clothes, walked right into its path. I was saying to myself, "What is

Mike doing here? It's Sunday." What a mess! As I was running back into the apartment, I could hear Mike shouting my name really loudly.

Minutes later, there was a knocking on the door. I just knew it was not one of the neighbors coming to say hello. My mother opened the door, and I heard my name repeatedly. The janitor told my mother what had happened and what had happened other times.

Mom called to me in an angry tone. I slowly walked to the front door. She yelled at me and started pulling my ear for causing an embarrassing incident. I could not deny it, so I had to apologize to him and help him clean up the mess that I caused. Mom yelled and said, "Don't you ever learn?"

So no more airmail deliveries, and because of my laziness, I had to take the trash down for a whole month, with no exceptions. Sometimes airmail is not the swiftest or best way.

We all looked forward to our birthdays; we were always well behaved. Mom would always invite some cousins, and we could invite a few close friends.

This was one of the few times we got to have junk food and soda, and even that was limited. Then we played games like pin the tail on the donkey and hide-and-seek. Even though we did not have the games and entertainment the children have today, we still had a blast.

Chapter 5

New Additions

Harry brought a kitten home; it was just about the Christmas season, so we all decided to call him Jingles. He became attached and close to Mom; he would sleep by her feet and get up when she did.

Mary had a habit of annoying him by either pulling his tail or his whiskers. Elephants do not forget, and neither did Jingles. Whenever she was barefoot, he would attack her feet and run off. The funny part was Mary could not understand why Jingles only attacked her. As one can see, Mary did not just annoy people.

Harry worked in a local butcher shop while he went to night school. He always brought home fresh beef kidneys, which Jingles got to love. Sometimes I would give him food I did not finish. We tried giving him ordinary, everyday cat food, but he would just smell it and walk off.

He would stick his face in his bowl while we were trying to feed him. So we would separate him from his bowl until his food was ready.

I remember one morning I heard him make a crying sound. I looked under the bed and in the closet but could not locate him. Then we all started looking. Well, we finally located him. He was on the fire escape and was too afraid to walk back in because of the thin rails.

Jack went onto the fire escape and brought him back. He ran under the bed like a scared cat. We all figured he must have seen a pigeon on the fire escape and gone out through the open window.

Not noticing his surroundings, he slowly crawled onto the fire escape trying to sneak up on it. The pigeon must have seen him and flown off. When he realized where he was, he had frozen up. I knew then where that expression "scaredy-cat" came from.

One morning when I was putting on my shoes, I felt something. When I looked, I saw Jingles had left me a surprise. It was a dead mouse; everybody told me that meant he was showing his love. I could do without that kind of loving.

One day, when my friend Louis was over at my house, we had a little disagreement. I told Jingles to attack. He jumped on his back and was hanging on to him, not letting go. It was not until he drew blood that he let go. After that episode, Lou thought twice before disagreeing with me!

Mom brought a canary home; we said that was a nifty act with a cat in the house. Mom was determined to keep the bird, so we hung the cage in the living room. Now we all had a new job, and we took turns cleaning the cage.

It was one of my sisters' turns to clean the cage, and she forgot to close the door. All of sudden, we saw the bird escaping. Mom started shouting to shut all the windows and watch the cat.

Jingles spotted the bird, licked his lips, and started to pursue it. Harry grabbed Jingles and put him in the bathroom until we retrieved it. We finally caught it and put it back in the cage. After that, every time someone cleaned the cage, Jingles would watch and hope for another escape.

One night, while we were sleeping, I heard a noise coming from the living room. What caught my attention was I could hear the birdcage swinging. When I walked into the living room, I spotted Jingles hanging from the side of the cage.

It seems he had leaped from the top of the TV and just managed to get his claws into the fabric cover that Mom had put over the cage every night, leaving him in an awkward position. Everybody woke up and came to see what had happened. He gave us a look like, "Oops, caught in the act."

I guess cats will be cats. We had to move the television farther away. We hoped he would not repeat his performance.

When Harry worked at the butcher shop, I would go and get some samples of freshly sliced cold cuts. My favorite was the one they called New England-style bologna. It was bologna with large chunks of ham in it. I also enjoyed regular bologna, especially when I could fry it in a pan. It smelled and tasted like a hot dog. Mom would yell at me because I would burn the pan and make a mess. Every time I would cook, Jingles would be there to get a taste of whatever I was preparing. One thing I learned was if it was not fresh, he would just smell it and walk off. One could not ask for a better food taster!

Sleeping with my brothers in one bed was always difficult. Sneaking out of the bedroom wasn't much easier. This one night, I was hungry because I had not liked what Mom had made for supper. So after everybody went to bed, I sneaked into the kitchen as quiet as a mouse. I had to be careful because the new refrigerator had a light, which would shine into Mom's bedroom.

I was being extremely careful and quiet while opening the refrigerator, trying not to wake anyone. All of a sudden, Jingles came up behind me and startled me. I was holding a jar of peanut butter and the milk. It all fell on the ground and made a racket. He ran off, scared just like a cat.

With the noise, everybody woke up. All the lights were turned on, and there I was caught red-handed in the middle of a disaster. The first voice I heard was my mother's yelling, "What are you doing?"

I told her, "I was hungry."

She went on saying there was plenty of food that I should have eaten at supper. I got no sympathy. I just helped her clean up the mess.

I went back to bed still hungry. Jingles was sticking his head out from under one of the beds, looking to see if it would be safe to come out. I think Mom had Jingles on kitchen patrol.

Harry usually came home from work at the same time, but this one Saturday night, he was really late. When he finally got home, he told us the butcher store had been robbed. What made it scary was the robber locked them all in the walk-in refrigerator while he was cleaning out the register.

Luckily for them, one of the brothers forgot something and came back. It could have been a long, long cold weekend, because the store was not open on Sunday.

Mom would make a lot of homemade items from scratch, whether it was food or other things. She would spend hours making "Kolyva" cooked wheat (symbolizing the mixing of souls in heaven) for our dad's memorial service. The one item I remember well was the soap she made. She would spend hours making it just to save a few pennies. She also made Greek-style yogurt. Mom sometimes would even save the aluminum foil by washing it and reusing it; she would even sew our socks.

Mom was always looking for ways to economize. So when she found out about this new program called Green Stamps, there was no stopping her. Some of the different local merchants were giving them for purchases. Mom would collect them and redeem them for free gifts.

Mom got terribly upset when she received an increase in the rent for the amount of $5.00 a month. She was paying $26.50 a month. By today's standards, it does not sound like much, but it was a 20 percent increase. Mom was a worrier, and she was always concerned about how to make ends meet.

My brothers reassured her she did not need to worry, because everything would be okay. I noticed she would economize in other ways to adjust to the increase. Mom was a true believer and always felt if one could not afford it, one could do without it. If one wanted it that dreadfully, one should sacrifice something in return.

If the government followed some of these old-fashioned ideas, perhaps the country would be in better financial shape. Mom's favorite expression, especially when things were not going well, was: "We live in a fake world."

Chapter 6

New Adventures

When I turned twelve, I started to become more daring. That summer, we were going back to New Dorp. I wanted to explore the haunted house everybody seemed to fear. Over the years, I had gotten more into spooky and scary things. When I saw the summer crowd, I said, "When do we go to the haunted house?" Some of the local guys were surprised to hear me still talking about it.

After all these years, they were still reluctant to go. I was determined to check this house out. The same guy rambled on, "It's haunted. Believe me. Take my bike and see for yourself. You cannot miss it. Just leave the bike in my back yard."

That night, after supper, it was still light out, so I again asked who wanted to go. Nobody answered me. "Okay, I will go myself." I took his bike and went. I was a little nervous not knowing what to expect.

He was right; there it was, standing all by itself with tall weeds and a large sign saying, "No Trespassing." The house looked just like it was out of a scary movie. This was going to be even more adventurous than I'd first thought. It was starting to get dark, so I decided to come another day.

As I was leaving, I heard a noise coming from the direction of the house. I walked a little closer. I could have sworn I saw something looking through one of the cellar windows. As much as I liked scary things, it was freaking me out. I just took off.

The next day, I told the other guys what I saw. I asked again, "Who wants to go?"

Everybody got quiet. Then this girl said to me, "I would love to go."

I replied, "This is not for girls." I told them, "Okay, I'll go myself." I asked who had a flashlight that I could borrow.

This one kid said, "My dad has a lantern."

He got it for me, and I said, "Come with me."

He replied with a flat "Hell no."

I could not believe they were still afraid to go.

This time, I was going to walk. I decided to take a shortcut through some wooded areas. I went a little earlier, hoping to get to see what the heck was scaring them. I had an early supper; then I told my mother I was going to hang out with some of the boys. She gave me her usual remarks.

As I was getting closer, I could sense someone was following me. I just continued, keeping an eye open. When I got to the house, I did a little exploring before I entered. When I had been there last, the cellar door had been closed. Now, I found it open; something was not right. Again, I heard something in the woods behind me, and I yelled out, "Who's there?"

I slowly walked to the house and discovered that the front door was not locked. I went inside and looked around, and I saw signs that someone had been there recently. Then I heard footsteps coming up to the front door; I quickly hid behind a doorway.

I saw the door opening, and I was ready to throw the lantern. It was the girl who had wanted to come with me. I shouted, "You scared me half to death!"

She replied, "I was also curious to see if the house is haunted and if ghosts exist."

Well, as long as we were there, I thought, we might as well thoroughly explore the house. We walked slowly, dodging some cobwebs. I saw stairs. I told her to stay put and I would check upstairs. She said, "No, I am too scared."

I whispered to her, "Okay," and we both walked up the squeaky stairs. Most of the rooms were just empty and full of cobwebs.

It was starting to get dark. I said we should start heading home. She agreed, and we started walking down the stairs, when all of a sudden, we heard a loud noise. I could not tell exactly where the sound was coming from. She whispered, "I think it came from the cellar."

After the noise, we both ran down the stairs. Her foot fell through one of the steps that was rotted. As I was trying to get her foot free, that noise was getting louder. I slowly pulled her foot out. Her sneaker came off and fell into the cellar.

She let out a scream, "My mother is going to kill me. She just bought these sneakers. I have to get it, no matter what."

I looked through the hole with the lantern. I spotted the sneaker; by this time, it was quite dark. We had no clue what time it was. We found the door to the cellar next to what was once a kitchen. It was either locked or stuck. She kept screaming, "We got to get my sneaker!"

I said, "Relax, we'll get it."

I was hoping that door outside was another entrance to the cellar.

She kept holding on to me, saying, "I'm scared."

I said, "You should have stayed home."

When we got to the side of the house, I noticed that same door I'd seen earlier was now closed. I said, "That's funny." Not wanting to frighten her, I was thinking to myself, *There is clearly someone else here.* I was somewhat concerned, not knowing what I'd find in the cellar besides her sneaker.

I slowly opened the door with her help. I took the lantern and shined it into the basement. I was checking around extremely carefully.

Then we heard the noise again. It was coming from the cellar. She said, "I guess the house is haunted."

I told her, "Ghosts do not make noises like that." My heart was racing. Not knowing what to expect, I yelled out, "Who's there?" When we got into the cellar, I noticed a dim light from under a doorway. I was thinking to myself, *Why is there a light in an empty house?*

She said, "I see my sneaker," and she hopped down to get it. While she was putting it on, I was shouting, "Hurry up!" All of a sudden, this "thing" grabbed her hand, and she screamed. Without thinking twice, I hit whatever it was with the lantern, knocking it down, and we both ran like there was no tomorrow.

We ran so quickly from the house, never looking back. When we got back, we were huffing and puffing. I asked her if she was okay, because I was still shaking.

Once we had both settled down, we went home. My mother had a fit when she saw me sneaking into the house. "Do you realize what time it is?"

I just went to bed saying nothing. The problem was I could not sleep thinking about what we had just encountered.

I told the guys about the experience. "We warned you it was haunted," they said. I loved scary things, but I did not believe that ghosts would grab someone. I was curious to see what had happened, but I did not want to push my luck.

When I saw the girl, she asked me what that was last night. I said, "It was no ghost." I just kept my distance, as much as I wanted to understand the whole story.

Shortly thereafter, we all found out the truth about the so-called haunted house. It seems two dirtbags had been living in the cellar. One of them tried to lure a young girl to the cellar, but she managed to escape. Her parents reported the incident to the police.

So the mystery of the haunted house was finally uncovered. Now the haunted house was just an old house. It was later torn down to make room for new housing. As we got older, the whole area changed, so that ended the summer getaway.

Back in the city, my friends and I would go places that we were forbidden to go. I guess being boys, we did not pay attention. We enjoyed going to different places, like the United Nations Plaza, the Fifth Avenue Library, the Chrysler Building, Grand Central Station. Everything was just a short walking distance from where we lived. We were always getting into all types of mischief.

Grand Central Station became our favorite spot. It was so vast there was so much to see and explore. It was like a city in itself; there were so many different kinds of shops and restaurants.

In the lower portion of the terminal, we discovered a section where we could echo our voices through this long, long walkway that went under the city streets.

We would sneak into different parts of the terminal that were off-limits to the public and play hide-and-seek. One of our favorite places was the top of the terminal; we all called it Frankenstein Tower. We gave it that name because it was always on the dark side. We also discovered this large wooden box that looked like a casket.

We were always exploring different parts of the terminal and always found something new. I will never forget one of my friends discovered this doorway. We came to find out that it went down into a dark, cold, abandoned underground station.

When we first opened the door, it was too dark to see anything. We needed flashlights in order to explore what we could not see. It was getting late, so we decided to select another day.

My brother Jack had this flashlight with a spotlight on it, which was perfect for this adventure. The problem was I had to sneak it out of the house, which was sometimes difficult because my sisters were always watching me like a hawk. They always wanted to know my whereabouts and would tell on me, especially my sister Mary.

I took charge, and once we got somewhat organized, we started our adventure. I was leading the way. All of a sudden, we all felt this tremendous blast of cold air, and the door slammed closed. The last guy ran yelling, "I'm getting out of here." He ran back to the door. He started yelling, "I cannot open the door!"

I got a little nervous myself, and I cautiously walked back to the door to check it out. The door would not open. It was like something or someone had put a lock on the outside. The one guy shouted out, "What do we do now?"

I said, "There must be another way out."

One of my friend's startled me, causing me to drop my flashlight. I could see the flashlight from a distance, so we went to retrieve it. We found another door when we got to the bottom. The same guy ran to the door to see if it was open.

I yelled out, "Wait! Let's be a little more careful this time." I opened the door, and I put the spotlight on. I moved the spotlight slowly, and we saw strange images. It was hard to explain. Then we heard strange sounds from afar.

The same guy was freaking out. I told him to shut up. It was cold and damp; plus it even had a musty smell. It was even freaking me out. I did not say a word. I just pretended like it was nothing and kept my composure. The door had brought us to an old train station that looked like it had been out of service for many years. We saw signs dating back to the early 1900s.

Then we came across an old abandoned train that looked as if it had been in a serious accident. I spotted one of the doors open. I slowly walked in and checked around.

Some of the seats were on top of each other, and some were still intact. Then out of nowhere, I could have sworn I saw someone or something sitting in one of the seats. I yelled to my friends, and they all came running. I told them there was someone sitting in the front seat. The one guy yelled, "Are you crazy?"

When I looked again, that person or thing had disappeared. I said, "Let's get out of here; something is not right." As we were about ready to walk out, the door slammed closed. We felt that same blast of cold air. The same guy began screaming, "We are trapped, and we are going to die in here!"

Again I told him to shut up. We kept walking from car to car looking to find a way out. One of my friends shouted, "I see an opening!" And we all squeezed through this small window.

We kept walking to the end of this decrepit, cold, damp station looking for another way out. That same, musty smell was getting stronger. Then, all of a sudden, we saw people walking toward us.

I yelled, "What the heck are those?" We could not even see their faces. It was so dark, it created the impression they were faceless.

Now I did not believe in ghosts, but what the heck was that? We started running. One of my friends tripped and hit this door, and it slammed open. We stopped to investigate, and we saw stairs heading up.

We were hoping this would be another exit, so we quickly ran up the stairs. It seemed like forever before we got to the top. When we finally got there, we started searching for a doorway, but with no luck.

We were all huffing and puffing, as we came upon a dead end. We felt all around and used the flashlights but could not find a door or any other way out.

We could hear vehicle traffic on the other side of the wall. We all started shouting, but nobody responded. Again, I was thinking to myself, *If ghosts do not exist, what the heck was that we all saw?*

I started banging on the wall using the flashlight. I was even getting scared now. I kept thinking to myself, *Those individuals, or whatever they were, we saw are going to follow us up the stairs.* I continued banging even harder. All of a sudden, we saw daylight coming through a crack.

When we saw daylight, we all started banging even harder. With all the banging, we had made a hole large enough for us to squeeze out. The opening took us behind the terminal to a street where we saw cars and trucks whizzing by.

It felt terrific to see daylight and get a breath of fresh air. We got our bearings and ran all the way home, not looking back.

My brother's flashlight looked like a truck had run over it. I got it back into the house without anybody seeing me. I just waited for him to see it before I would admit anything. He never mentioned it, so I never brought it up.

We found out more about that mystery tunnel; it seems there was a terrible train crash in the early 1900s. The accident killed and trapped many people. Maybe it was their spirits we saw that day. We kept going back to Grand Central terminal to venture to other parts, but we never attempted to enter that damp and musky-smelling tunnel station again. It was as if fate was telling us, "Do not push your luck."

Just before school started, Mom took us shopping for new clothing. I would bug my mother to buy me a pair of PF Flyer sneakers. It took a little convincing, but after a while, she came around. With my new sneakers, I thought I could run a four-minute mile.

Chapter 7

Still Learning

All my friends had their heroes; mine was General Douglas MacArthur. We even shared the same birthday. In my eyes, he was one of the great generals. He had foresight that could have changed history. When President Truman fired him, I could see the world was changing for the worse. My mother would scold me when I called the president a dummy. I will always remember his famous quotes, "I shall return," and "Old soldiers never die; they just fade away."

One of my friends worked part-time in this deli-style restaurant; his job was only to make deliveries. There were a few days when he could not work, and he would ask me to cover for him. The only income was from the tips. I would deliver to many local offices, but the best was when I delivered to the TV studio Of WPIX, in the *Daily News* Building.

I would deliver to the front desk, and they would come and get their food. Some days, there was no one at the desk, so I went directly to the studios.

After I had delivered the orders, I would sneak around to where they were filming. I got to meet a lot of famous celebrities. I will always remember I literally ran into Bela Lugosi, dressed as Dracula. He gave me that favorite remark, "I want to drink your blood." Other times, I met Larry Harmon, who played Bozo the Clown; William Boyd, known as Hopalong Cassidy, and his sidekick Gabby Hayes; and my hero Captain Video. This was fun, even if I did not get any tips.

I always looked forward to the Fourth of July; the older guys would put on a fireworks display. Most of them would do it in an orderly fashion, but there were the few who would take it further. They would throw them into the hallways of an apartment house and even place them in a hobo's shoe while he was sleeping. While playing with fireworks, one of the guys somehow managed to lose a finger. So that ended my desire to play with fireworks!

My friends and I would always find things to keep us occupied and kept out of trouble, most of the time. We would make these wooden swords and fight each other just like Zorro did in the movies. We also played games like hide-and-seek, Johnny on a pony, Ring a Larry-O, tag, and London bridge.

My sisters and their friends would play games like hopscotch and jump rope. Sometimes to annoy them, we would jump in while they were playing.

My friend Louis and I were always doing things together. Most every Saturday, we'd go to the Y; afterward, we would have lunch and then go to the Museum of Natural History. We spent hours just admiring the individual exhibits. It was so vast, in all the times we went, we could never see everything.

The older guys would turn on the fire hydrants when it was hot. The police, or sometimes the firemen, would turn them off, and no sooner than they did, they would turn them on again. It got so out of hand they put locks on the fire hydrants.

We would all play stickball. Because of the location, only one group could play at a time, so the older guys would chase us when they wanted to play. When we could play, we played in the street around the corner from where we lived. The street was one of the exits for the Midtown Tunnel, and because of that, it was a fairly busy street.

Sometimes, the older guys would take the bat and ball. So when that happened, we had to get another bat and ball. When it was my turn, I had no other choice but to get my mother's broom. I had to saw off the handle and then get rid of the straw end, before Mom or anyone else could catch me. I felt guilty doing it. Mom did not realize the broom was missing until she needed to use it. Of course, she could not find it, and then she started yelling at my brother Jack. One day, Mom caught on and realized that I was the one. She yelled and said, "*Gel'eft*" (thief.)

Every Saturday afternoon, the trucks that delivered the Sunday newspaper would park waiting to have their trucks loaded where we usually played stickball. They would leave them unattended, and we would play hide-and-seek in and around the trucks. One of my nervier friends got into the driver's seat and decided to try to start the truck. I said, "Are you crazy?" No sooner had I said it than the truck leaped forward and hit another truck that was in front of it, pushing it into the middle of the intersection; after that, we all took off. He never tried that stupid maneuver again. They would also park the trucks that delivered these gigantic rolls of paper for the newspaper there. Somehow, some of the rolls got loose and rolled off the truck, almost crushing a car. The rumor was someone had removed the pieces of wood that kept the rolls in place.

My brother Jack was gifted with a good throwing arm. He could throw a hardball a full city block and hit a two-foot-by-two-foot box and almost always get the ball within the square. He also played on a baseball farm team as a pitcher. Harry and I would go several times to watch him play downtown just off the East River. He played until he was diagnosed with a slight heart problem. That ended any chances of him maybe going into the majors.

The neighborhood was just a large family. Everybody knew everybody. One of the fellows from our block named Rafael got lucky and got a part to play in a movie called *Blackboard Jungle*. We mostly all got along with each other; there was always the expectations. Just around the corner from where we lived was the "no-play zone." We were all banned from going anywhere near there, mainly because of some Hispanic wise guys.

As for ourselves, we were not wise guys or troublemakers. It all started when a few of them came around to our block. It seemed to always happen when we were not there. They would tease some of the girls. That was a no-no. When my sisters told me about it, I got even more irritated, so I got some of my friends together to pay them a visit. My sisters reminded me about what Mom had said about going there. I guess I was just being thickheaded.

We decided to go and bring it to a conclusion. When we first got there, no one was anywhere to be found. Then, all of a sudden, they came out of nowhere. Before we knew it, we were outnumbered two to one. One of my bigger friends shouted, "What's the problem? Why are you all bothering the girls?" We exchanged some words, and then suddenly some of them pulled out stick bats.

I yelled out, "What's with the bats?"

One of them swung his bat, and stupid me, not thinking, I put up my hand to grab it. Before I realized it, he hit my hand, and my middle finger blew up like a balloon. I must have gone crazy. I started hitting anybody that came near me. Then all hell broke out. Before we knew it, we all started slugging it out. Some older men who were working at the *Daily News* came and broke the fight up. After they had separated us, there were a few remarks exchanged as we were going back.

As I was walking into the house, Mom was coming out. How would I explain this? She had a fit when she saw my balloon-sized finger and wanted to know what had happened.

I knew if I told her the whole truth, I would get in trouble. I told her we were playing, and my finger got in the way of the bat. I was not totally lying.

It looked worse than it was, but Mom made me go to the emergency room just the same. They x-rayed my finger and told us there was no break. They taped it up and told me no sports for a few weeks.

Two of them came around to apologize and see how my finger was. At first, I thought they had come to cause problems. We chatted for a while, and I realized they were just like us. Everybody, including myself, had been labeled troublemakers. Some of my friends said I was being ignorant to have any affiliation with them. Another lesson I learned while I was growing up: do not label people because of their heritage or what others say.

Our neighborhood had its dramatic moments. One day, a horse got loose from its wagon and went stampeding, damaging cars. The police had no choice but to shoot it. One night, while watching TV, we heard gunshots. We all thought it was just a car backfiring. It seems one of the local policemen shot at a car because the man had driven off, while he was questioning him. The story was he had gotten shot in the hand, and it might have been self-inflicted. A *Daily News* truck somehow started rolling down Second Avenue while we were playing. It looked funny because we saw no driver, but then we took a second look. It plowed into some parked cars. It was a domino effect; by the time it had totally stopped, it had crushed several cars. Thank God nobody got injured.

Down the block, there was a shabby man. He looked mean. He would sit on this old rocking chair. For as long as I could remember, it seemed like he always wore the same suit. He also had this bulldog that even looked shabby. When I first saw him, I felt sorry for him. Then I learned he owned many apartment houses and was not as poor as I had originally thought.

I also came to realize he had a decent, charitable heart and would help many people in need. That old saying, "Do not judge a book by its cover," applied here.

Years later, just a few blocks from where we lived, a man named Fidel Castro was visiting and staying at a second-class hotel. Having heard about him on TV and in the newspapers, my friends and I were curious to see him. So we ran over to check him out. There were police barriers in front of the hotel, and many people demonstrating. We timed it just right, though. He was coming out of the car wearing these green military fatigues that looked liked he'd slept in them. For a guy in his thirties, he looked old.

The funny part was some of his associates were carrying live chickens into the hotel. We came to find out he had gotten evicted because of the live chickens. This could only happen in New York.

As the years rolled on, I could never understand how we could let a dictator take over a country just ninety miles off the coast. Yet, we would worry about other countries thousands of miles from the mainland. To this day, I'm trying to understand how politicians think; apparently, it is not with their heads.

Mom was always meeting new families; she had met this family who'd just come from Greece. They had two children: a son named Teddy and a daughter named Angie. Teddy was just a little younger than I was, and his sister was about Mary's age. Mom asked me to make him feel comfortable, because he had had no luck making new friends. They spoke Greek with only a limited amount of English. At first, my friends would tease him because of that. We became extremely close; he was like a younger brother.

Some of the older guys would get into a lot of serious misconduct. They would jump the turn slot on the elevated train stations, and they would do stupid things. They would unscrew lightbulbs from the train cars and throw them at passing vehicles. That was not serious enough though, because one day, they were stupid enough to uncouple one of the elevated train cars. The train had pulled into the Forty-Second Street station, and while it was letting passengers on and off, they separated the last car from the rest. So when the train pulled out, the last car just stayed behind. The engineer never realized it until the conductor notified him, and that was not until he was almost at the next station. It caused problems for passengers and the Interborough Rapid Transit.

The same guys would ride on the back of trolley cars and throw things at pedestrians. It took a deadly accident to wake them up. One day, when they were stupidly riding behind a trolley, one of them slipped and fell in front of another trolley going the opposite way. It is a shame that they had to learn the hard way.

Another question arose while I was growing up: why does it take a deadly mishap for people to learn? What ever happened to basic common sense? As I got older, I realized common sense was something that many people lacked.

It was not long after this that the trolley cars were replaced with buses, and soon after that, the Third Avenue el was being taken down.

Some of the trolley cars went to a Vienna, Austria, museum as part of the Marshall Plan foundation, which benefited the Austrian and American universities and academics.

After school, I would run over and watch them dismantle it, just like it was an Erector Set. The Third Avenue el was completed in 1878. In 1950, they started eliminating it in sections. The first section was the South Ferry "spur," which connected to Chatham Square. The next section was removed in 1955. It was from Chatham Square to 149th Street and was the main line. The final section was removed in 1973. This was the end of the Third Avenue el era.

Most of the train cars were being placed in the New York Harbor to help support the underwater canyons.

In 1940, just when I came into this world, the Second Avenue el was taken down. Most of the steel was given to Japan as a token of goodwill. Then, shortly thereafter, they gave it back to us by bombing Pearl Harbor.

Instead of removing the trolley tracks, they put blacktop over them. A short time later, after the cold weather and all the snow and ice, the tracks were coming through the surface, causing large potholes, which resulted in numerous accidents. They had no choice but to remove the tracks and resurface the streets again.

Talk about wasted taxpayer dollars! This sounds so familiar, and the shameful part is how some things do not change but remain the same. Dad always told me that during my life, I was going to see many changes. He was so right. The city was changing, and I always wondered if the city was changing for the better.

As I was growing up, there was discussion about the city constructing a Second Avenue subway. The years passed, and it was still just talk. It was not until the turn of the century that it became a reality. In 2007, they finally broke ground; it is expected to be completed in 2015.

One day, I was running home when one of the neighborhood dogs started chasing me. The dog leaped up and bit the lower part of my leg. Harry took me straight to the emergency room. They stitched me up, gave me a tetanus shot, and sent me home.

A short time later, the janitor's dog bit me. I was on my way to the hospital again; they were getting to know my name by then. Now when I see any dog, I think twice about running or even petting it.

Gypsies would come and go. They would take up residence in an empty store, just below the apartment house. I was always curious to see how they lived; I became friendly with this boy about my age. My mother scolded me when she found out that I was socializing with them.

I could not believe how they lived. Maybe it was because I did not understand their customs. I wanted to learn some of their traditions. Just like they appeared, they would disappear in the middle of the night, leaving no trace of them having ever been there.

Chapter 8

My Adolescent Years

In 1953, I was one out of five who would represent the city of New York. I guess it paid for me to go to the dentist regularly. I had won an award for having perfect teeth. One was selected from each of the boroughs; I would represent Manhattan. We all received awards from the mayor, Vincent Impellitteri, and we took pictures. Then to make it more rewarding, we had the honor of having lunch with the mayor.

Again, in 1954, I won the honor. This time it was with Mayor Robert Wagner Jr. Both times, my picture appeared in the *Daily News*, and I felt like a real celebrity. Just for the record, they were both Democrats—not that it mattered, or did it?

In 1954, one of my favorite ball players, Joe DiMaggio, married Marilyn Monroe. The first color twelve-inch TV went on sale too. It was only one thousand dollars. The first Burger King opened, and the first TV dinner was unveiled. A movie called *The Wild One* with Marlon Brando started a big trend. It seems many guys wanted to look "cool." So because of that, black leather jackets, blue jeans, white T-shirts, and dark sunglasses were selling off the shelves.

Mom had always wanted to become an American citizen as long as I could remember. She started going to classes, and we would help her on some of the questions.

She was cute the way she would give the answer in her broken English. We will never forget when she got her American citizenship papers. Mom was so excited, one would think she had graduated from an academy. We were all proud of her accomplishment.

When I turned fourteen and was just starting high school, I got a part-time job working for a local jeweler. I was earning sixty-five cents an hour and would work about fifteen to eighteen hours a week. I knew if my mother felt my job was hurting my schoolwork, she would definitely make me quit.

I had a few subjects I was doing poorly in, so I did not want Mom to see my report card. I told Harry about it; he said I better improve my grades for the next marking period. I'd take care of it right away, because Mom was no dummy and she would get suspicious eventually.

As much as we loved Mom, we sometimes took advantage of her because she could not comprehend English that well. So we had to be careful how we handled each detail.

I remember when a company, E. J. Korvettes, had just opened. It was one of the first discount stores to make its debut, which put a hurt on many merchants.

He was forced to lower many of his prices to stay in the retail business as well as try to compete with them. What saved him typically were his jewelry and watch repairs.

My new job was fun; I would wait on customers and do some stocking and cleaning. He later taught me a little about different types of jewelry and how to identify diamonds and other precious gems.

There were so many repairs that there were not enough hours in the day for him to repair all of them himself. So part of my job was to take these different items to be fixed at various merchants downtown. I would later pick up the completed work either the same day or on my next trip.

One thing I did learn about the retail business was the big profits that were made in jewelry and watch sales. So whenever you see sales where they offer up to 70 percent off, doesn't that make you wonder?

I can still remember, especially now, this old-time jeweler who bought and sold precious metals like gold, silver, etc. He said, "Buy gold now while you are young." If I did, I would be an exceptionally rich man. At that time, gold was going for $35.00 an ounce.

I would get a little nervous sometimes because there were times I carried a lot of expensive watches, jewelry, and sometimes even diamonds, which were worth hundreds of dollars.

Because of the Christmas holidays, I was working many more hours, and Mom was getting upset. She told me I was putting in too many hours, and I was neglecting my schoolwork. I explained it was that time of the year and we were extremely busy. I promised her that I would have a satisfactory report card come the next marking period.

She said, "By the way, I do not remember seeing your last report card."

I changed the subject and lucked out because she did not say anything else about it.

Harry was so right, and I felt guilty. I had to make sure that I improved my grades for the next marking period.

Come Christmas week, I had earned about twenty dollars. It felt fantastic, because for the first time, I could buy everybody a gift. So I took my whole pay, which my boss always put into an envelope, and I placed it in my pocket and went shopping.

I was taking my time, buying what I felt each would like. I got all my shopping finished and proceeded to pay for them. The cashier rang up my order, and the total came to just under twenty dollars.

When I reached for the envelope, nothing came out except some loose change and some thread. I checked it again and again. I could not believe I had lost my whole pay. I wanted to cry. The clerk was shouting at me because I was holding up the line.

With tears in my eyes, I told her I had lost my money. She started shouting again, asking how I was going to pay for this without money. I felt like my whole world had come crashing down, and I slowly walked out empty-handed. I could not understand how careless I had been.

I became terribly depressed, and my boss could sense something. I hesitated to tell him, but I told him just the same. He said, "That is a shame, but things will work out."

Christmas Eve day, the store was extremely busy with last-minute shoppers. He told me he had had a record-breaking Christmas season. He said to me, "Why not leave early?" so I could enjoy my holiday. He handed me an envelope just like he always did and said, "Merry Christmas." I was quite surprised because he was Jewish.

I shouted out, "Thank you and Merry Christmas!" and I left.

I was extremely happy that he had given me a Christmas gift. I looked into the envelope, and I pulled out a crisp twenty-dollar bill; my eyes lit up. Now I could go buy gifts for everybody. I carefully put the money in my wallet. Now, from that moment on, I realized I worked too hard to lose money that easily.

Every store I tried to shop at was closing early because it was Christmas Eve. Now that I had the money, I could not even spend it. I got upset again, so I started heading home.

I saw this sign that read, "Last-minute Shoppers"; it was the local Whelan's drugstore. I hoped they were still open, so I ran quickly. When I got to the door, the man said to me, "I'm sorry, but we are closing." I begged him to let me purchase a few things. The man hesitated and then said, "Okay, please, shop fast."

I thanked the man, and I shopped so fast, not realizing what I was buying or for whom. When the man rang up my order, I had spent less than ten dollars. I wanted to purchase more, but the man gave me a negative attitude. Deciding not to push my luck, I stayed with what I had purchased.

I ran home and wrapped all the gifts before anybody could see them. I now had to decide which gift would be suitable for whom. At least I had been able to get everybody a gift, and that made me feel warm.

Christmas morning, when we were opening the gifts, my brothers teased me about the gifts I had bought them. As for my sisters, they were happy that I had gotten them a gift. I explained to my brothers that it was last-minute shopping. It was this or zip. I also realized it was not the amount of the gift but the thought that counted.

We had the usual sumptuous Christmas dinner, and as usual, we all stuffed ourselves until the next holiday.

Every year, just after New Year's, most families threw out the Christmas trees. So the older guys would collect all the tress they could get their hands on and put them in a towering pile and burn them.

One year, it got so out of control they almost started a house on fire. It was lucky the fire department was just around the corner. The police also arrived and warned them no more Christmas-tree fires or someone was going to be arrested.

Since Mom and Dad followed the Eastern Orthodox calendar, we kept the tree up until January 6 to celebrate "Little Christmas."

The worst concern about leaving the tree up so long was it was drying out. A lot of the needles would be falling off. To make matters worse, by the time we took it down the five flights of stairs, more of the needles would fall off. Mom always had one of us sweep up the falling needles.

I enjoyed going to the Rockefeller Center during the Christmas season to see the enormous Christmas tree. I always became mesmerized whenever I went. Did you know there are over five miles of lights wrapped around the tree? I'd hate to have that electric bill. At last count, the tallest tree stood at one hundred feet in 1948. The first tree at Rockefeller Center stood up in 1931. Dad had told me during World War II, the tree was not lit to conserve electricity.

I also enjoyed watching the ice skaters. I would walk over to the Radio City Music Hall, hoping to get a glance at the show. Unfortunately, it was not till years later that I saw the show. I came to find out the Rockettes first appeared the Christmas of 1932.

It was report card time again. I managed to raise my grades in the subjects in which I had been doing poorly, thanks to my cousin Athena. She always came to my rescue whenever I needed that extra help.

We would play ball just about all year round, especially when the weather cooperated. We discovered this baseball field that was near the United Nations library. It was only for softball, but we would play hardball. We also found out that a permit was required.

To get a game in, we would go bright and early. This one Saturday, we lucked out and completed a game against some other guys from another neighborhood. We had two men on with two outs; we were down by one run in the last inning. I was up, and I had struck out twice before. My team was screaming for a hit. I'll never forget I hit the ball so hard it went sailing over the fence and right into a window at the library.

All we could hear was the glass breaking. Minutes later, the United Nations police came to investigate. Everybody all of a sudden pointed the finger at me. I had gotten the winning run, but now all of sudden, I was the bad guy.

The regular police came while we were leaving. My friend Louis said to them, "Some other guys just left." After they questioned us, we just left. We lucked out, thanks to my friend's quick thinking. I knew then why only softball was permitted.

Saturday, Mom did her main shopping at the local Safeway supermarket. Since it was a Saturday, I would sometimes sleep late. Mom had this two-wheeled cart that she used to transport her groceries. There were times she would have additional groceries, especially when it was any holiday. Mom was well organized; she had a routine. She would ring the doorbell from downstairs or even call out my name. I would then go downstairs to help with the groceries. Sometimes I would go down wearing my pajamas, and Mom of course would yell at me.

Getting the mail was always annoying; we all took turns doing it, because it meant walking down five flights of stairs and five up. Sometimes when we were playing, we would shout from downstairs for the key just to save those extra five flights. Mom was skeptical about dropping it because it might land in the sewer drain, which it did a few times.

We had the shiniest mailboxes in the neighborhood; thanks to Mike the janitor, who would polish them until you could see your reflection.

Compared to my brothers, I was unusually short for my age. For years, while we were growing up, a lot of my clothes were hand-me-downs.

One of my hand-me-downs was a PT coat. I loved that coat. I never wanted to give it up, even when it got frayed. Mom was always trying to throw it out. I would just recover it and then hide it from her. It was a no-win in the long run. Mom always won.

Mom several times had no choice but to buy clothes, as I was growing out of mine. Knowing Mom could not always afford to purchase everything I needed, I did something I would regret. When we went shopping this one day, I swapped my old, frayed belt for a new one. Isn't that called recycling?

Somehow, Mom found out, and she gave me an awful beating using that same belt on me. She said I should be ashamed of myself for doing a terrible act like that. Mom and I went back and paid for the belt, which I had stupidly taken. Another lesson: if you take something, you should be prepared for the consequences.

When I attended high school, I met many different students. A few of them that I came in contact with were quite different from the friends I had made growing up. I have to admit I was exceedingly naive in my new school environment.

There was this one shabby-looking guy who offered me a cigarette, better known as a joint. Mom always hated anything related to smoking, which made me think twice, and my brothers had warned me about matters like this. This, of course, made me even more cautious, so I always rejected it.

Again, he approached me and said, "Don't be a drag." He said I would feel terrific after one. I just went on saying, "No."

He was trying to get me, as well as others, hooked on it by offering free smokes. Then I discovered other guys were pushing other drugs. I kept as far from them as possible. It was unbelievable how many students were hooked on different drugs.

Didn't the teachers and the office staff see this? After a while, he gave up on me. I still avoided him like the plague. My brother Jack then told me the reason they called drugs dope was because "dopes used them." I think getting superb, sound advice from your family does have a more positive outcome.

I'll never forget this one individual, who was much bigger than I was, constantly bullied me. One day in the school cafeteria, I tried to ignore him while I was buying my lunch. He went as far as tripping me. My food and drink went all over. I just picked up my tray and cleaned up the mess. I did not want to get into an argument or maybe even a fight. I went outside to the field area and sat down. I had to cool down.

As I was sitting there, he came out and started up again. I could hear my heart racing. Then it happened: he called me a nasty name with the word *mother* in it. That was all I had to hear, and with my Greek temper, I went after him like there was no tomorrow. I did not realize what I had done until someone told me later. It seems I hit him so hard in the face he went flying into the fence. They had to call first aid because he was out cold.

When the smoke cleared, they notified my mother that I was going to be expelled. I tried to explain I was just defending myself from his constant verbal harassment. They said I broke the rule, and they were making no exceptions. What bothered me was there were students selling drugs and getting away with it. Here I was, just defending myself, and I got expelled. What is wrong with that picture?

Mom was terribly upset and gave me a lecture on fighting. I tried to explain, but it was a no-win. I had to find another school to attend, which was difficult. I was rather glad I was leaving this school because of the other problems that I had experienced. After carefully checking my options, I finally got one that would take me.

On my first day, I was in the dean's office getting the riot act read to me. I tried to explain what had happened, but he could care less. He told me I was on a sixty-day trial to prove that I was not a troublemaker.

I did not believe what I had to go through to defend my self-respect. I was not in my new school more than a few days before somehow the word got out that I was a troublemaker and all I got was negative remarks.

Two seniors confronted me in the hall, and they started to pick on me. I remembered what the dean had told me, so I kept my composure and tried to ignore them. It was not getting any better, and it seemed to be the same wise guys.

One morning, while I was going to my homeroom class, the same two guys approached me again. They continued with their harassment. I had just about had it. My Greek temper was at its boiling point, so I lashed out at them and told them loudly to "keep off."

From nowhere, this gargantuan African-American fellow came to my rescue. He said in a firm voice, "Is there a problem?" They quickly backed off and left without saying another word.

He said, "I have been noticing that you are being picked on quite a bit."

I told him, "In a way, you might have saved me from almost being suspended or perhaps expelled." I thanked him and explained what had happened.

We were in the same grade, just different homerooms. From that day, we became friends. It was surprising because all of a sudden, nobody seemed to pick on me.

I was getting to enjoy my new school once things settled down. I was also keeping an eye open in case I came across the drug problem. I came to realize the way to beat the drug problem was just a simple "no."

In my second year, I made a lot of new friends and even got close with the dean. He apologized for the way he had treated me when I first came. He told me he learned something new: "Don't always judge people on what others may say."

I'll never forget the year 1955 when the Dodgers beat the Yankees for the World Series. Being a Manhattan boy in a Brooklyn school did not go over too well, especially at this time. I had to get out of Brooklyn if I wanted to stay healthy. I never saw so much craziness before with some of the things they did.

They even tried to block the Manhattan Bridge so vehicles couldn't enter Brooklyn. They went as far as making a dummy that looked like a Yankee ball player. They put a noose around its neck and then hung it from the entrance of the bridge.

All businesses and schools were closed to celebrate the occasion. One thing I did learn was not to mention the word *Yankee* or being a fan.

When the Dodgers played their last game at Ebbets Field on September 24, 1957, it ended an era. I never saw so many disappointed classmates. When the Giants played their last game at the Polo Grounds, also in 1957, I did not take it that badly. Maybe, because the new baseball team, called the Mets, played in the Polo Grounds until the 1963-year season. They moved to their new (Shea) stadium across in Queens. In 1964, the Polo Grounds were taken down to make room for new housing.

We all had habits, some decent and some bad. My brother Harry had an unhealthy habit of smoking, and Mom had a strong feeling that he smoked. Harry knew better than to try to bring the cigarettes into the apartment. He would hide them behind this mirror in the lobby. It was like Mom had this psychic power the way she found them. She would take them and crush them angrily.

I was not a regular smoker. I did it for other reasons. When I was about sixteen, my friend Gregg and I thought smoking a pipe would be neat. Plus we thought it made us look sophisticated and older.

It was just my luck I was heading home from Gregg's house one cold afternoon, smoking my pipe. As I was walking, I spotted my mother at a distance walking toward me. So without thinking, I stuck the pipe in my overcoat pocket still burning.

My mother stopped and started talking to me. Before I realized it, the pipe had burned right through my pocket and landed on the ground, making a loud sound. She asked, "What is that?"

I immediately said, "It is my friend Gregg's pipe. I'm holding it for him."

She must have believed me, because she never said another word about it.

A few days later, my friend Gregg called me and said, "Thanks for getting me in trouble." He told me his mother had seen my mother in church, and she told her about the pipe.

I told him what had happened, and that it was the first thought that came to me. I said, "What are friends for if we cannot blame each other?"

When our cat Jingles died, I cried like a baby. It was like losing a member of the family. For the few years he lived, it was amazing how he brought tranquility amongst us.

Mom, being old-fashioned, was not too thrilled when Harry began dating an Italian girl from the neighborhood. Harry told Mom he'd broken up with her, hoping to get her in a better frame of mind. I wondered if she had been Greek if Mom would have felt different!

The same restaurant I had borrowed napkins from years earlier, I came to find out, was owned by two Greek brothers. I got to meet them; their names were Andy and Ernie, and we became friendly. They gave me a job before school. I was to write the specials on the menu board. It did not take long, and I would have a quick breakfast. Mom got upset that I was eating there too often and felt it was not healthy.

I had saved enough money for my new bike, and this time, I made sure I had my mother's consent. Even though, I had her okay, I could feel she was not totally thrilled. My new bike was not anything fancy. In fact, I bought one of the lowest cost ones I could get, especially after what had happened last time.

My friends and I would ride our bikes around the neighborhood and also to Central Park. After a while, it was getting monotonous. I felt it was time to discover new territory, so I suggest something unusual, like going to New Jersey. There was a ferryboat, which would take us across the river, and the fare was just under twenty-five cents each way.

My friends thought I was crazy, but I said, "What is the difference if we go to New Jersey or Central Park. After convincing them, we decided to go on this new adventure.

Mom questioned me when she saw that I had packed a sandwich and snack. We did not dare tell our parents exactly where we were going; we just said we were going riding. Again, Mom made her famous comment, "*Ta matia sou dekatesita*" (Have fourteen eyes), and told me not to be too long.

The ferry ride was only a few minutes; we checked the schedule and found out it ran on the hour up until sunset.

When we got to the Jersey side, we had to ride up these hilly and winding roads. We must have traveled a mile or two along the Jersey side admiring the Manhattan skyline.

One of the guys said, "Let's ride up to Palisades Amusement Park."

I said, "For someone who did not want to go, now you want to go even further." I added, "Not today. Let's save it for another time."

We had lunch while we were enjoying the view of the city. We started heading back to catch the next ferry. Going home was a lot faster; it was all downhill. We were going so fast for a short time we were passing cars up.

My one friend had a speedometer on his bike. He shouted out we were nearing fifty miles per hour. I said, "We better slow down. That is extremely fast to be safe." I slowed down to a safer speed, but the others kept going at a high speed. I shouted out, "Slow down!" but before I knew it, they were out of sight.

As soon as they saw me, they called me a "slow poke." Seconds later, this police, car drove up to them. The officer got out and started yelling. He said, "Are you guys trying to kill yourselves?" He wanted to know where we lived and how old we were.

The officer threatened to impound their bikes. I spoke with him and asked him, "Please, give them just one more chance. It was my idea about coming across the river, please." He was polite about it, but told us all next time, he would run us in and then call our parents. I thanked him again.

As the ferry was pulling out, I was saying that because of this incident, we had missed the ferry. I lashed out and said, "Well, was it worth speeding? Where did it get us? This only proves rushing gets one nowhere faster." Nobody said anything. I knew my mother would be wondering where I had been all these hours.

When I got home, I quietly walked into the house; everybody was out. I had lucked out, so I washed up and watched some TV.

Mom came in with my sisters and did not say a word. Shortly afterward, Mary started up and asked where I had I been all day. She got Mom curious. I said, "I was out riding my bike with my friends." This was extremely typical of Mary; she was always stirring up the pot.

I had met this pretty girl at my church. She was just about my age. The problem was she lived in New Jersey. I asked to see her again, but being so far away, she was wondering how I could get to her house. I said I would come with my bike. I asked her, "How does 11:00 a.m. next Saturday sound?"

She said, "Are you insane? All the way from the city?"

I told her that I always enjoyed riding my bike long distances; it was a healthy workout.

It must have been puppy love. She gave me directions from the town's welcome sign, but I still got a road map. It was about sixteen miles one way.

Come Saturday morning, I told my mother I was going to play with my friends. She asked why I was wearing my dressy clothes. I would only get them dirty. As much as I did not want to lie, I told her I was going to hang out. Then she said, "Do not be too long."

I started my adventure. The first part was taking the ferry. I double-checked the schedule just to be sure it had not changed. I was making excellent time when all of a sudden I hit this pothole. I went flying and landed on some grass. My pants were full of grass stains, and I had also torn them.

I had lost some time, so I kept pedaling my way, saying to myself, "I hope it is all worth it." I had purchased a speedometer especially for this trip.

I finally saw the welcome sign. She had given directions, but nothing was the way she had explained.

I stopped to get better directions, only to find out I was on the other side of town. I was due to meet her at 11:00 a.m., and it was almost noon. I finally got to her house only to discover there was nobody home. She mostly likely thought I was not coming since I was so late. I was talking to myself, feeling like a real jerk. I was thinking, *Now what?*

After waiting a short time, I decided to head home. This car pulled up, and a gentleman stepped out. I explained to him who I was, and that I was meeting Maryann. He replied that he had just gotten back from playing golf and had no clue where everybody was. He said I was welcome to wait until she got back. He offered me a soda, and we sat on the porch and chatted. It was getting late, and I thanked him for his hospitality. He was sorry that I had come so far just to miss her.

I started my trip back home. I was not ten minutes on the road when I realized I had forgotten to put my safety clasp on the bottom my pant legs. Sure enough, they got caught on the chain.

Not wanting to rip my pants, I carefully got off the bike. I was hoping to free the pants, but no luck. I had only one option: to cut them free. To make matters worse, I had grease on my hands as well as my pants. There was nothing I could do at this point but continue heading home.

I was trying to catch the ferry; otherwise, I would have to wait. I could not help thinking about the police officer who stopped my friends.

I kept my speed down, thanks to my new speedometer. I made it to the terminal just in time. While I was on the ferry, I was thinking to myself, *How do I explain this? I look like a wreck.*

I managed to sneak home without my mother seeing me. It was just my luck that my sister Mary saw me. I pleaded with her not to tell Mom anything. Thanks to Mary, I got a sound scolding.

As for the wasted trip, I never found out what exactly happened. I did learn something; sometimes you should listen but never lie to your mother.

Chapter 9

The Years Roll By

Back in the early fifties, our first cousin George came from Greece on a student visa. My brother Jack and George grew up in Greece. They were about the same age. I would always tease George about his nose. Our front door had frosted glass, which gave a shadow image. His facial profile stood out, giving his nose an even a longer look. So when I answered the door, I would shout out, "It's cousin George." Because of that, my brothers and sisters would start doing the same. Mom would yell at us for always making that sarcastic remark.

My brothers and Cousin George would hang out together. I was too young to get involved with their social activities. Even though Harry was also younger, his size made up for it, and many times, he got away with it.

George most always was at the house for Sunday dinner and all the holidays. Over the years, I got to love George as another older brother. George had met this pretty girl named Helene.

As usual, Mom was not too thrilled about it, because she was not Greek. Mom had a name for these girls, "*a cène*" (stranger, not Greek). This was extremely typical of most Greek parents. After they were married, Helene fit right in, just like family.

When I was getting into my upper-teens, I did not attend a lot of our relatives' weddings and other affairs. Most of the time, I would be involved with my personal activities, which fell on the same day. Mom got upset with me when I stopped going. I just felt my social life was my own to enjoy.

As I got older, I realized Mom was right to feel the way she did. I came to realize these are times in life one can never relive. This was what made life more rewarding for a family.

Harry was giving Mom a significant chunk of his paycheck. So he decided to get a part-time job at a local liquor store, so he could save money to buy a car.

Harry and Cousin George had bought a car together without Mom knowing about it. At that time it was compulsory to have insurance when you are less than twenty-five years of age. Harry figured he'd put it under Mom's name. He had her signature down to a science. So he had to be careful because he did not want her to find out about the car.

He would keep the car at his boss's house in the Bronx and take the train whenever he wanted to use it. One night, when he had no night school, he went for a joyride.

While he was out, he hit a parked car and lost his bumper. Being young and brave and thinking nobody saw him, he took off. He returned the car back to his boss's house and went home.

When he came home, there were two detectives questioning Mom about the accident. Harry had not realized the license plate was on the missing bumper. Mom was saying, "What car?" in her broken English.

Harry walked in as though nothing had happened. When Mom saw him, she grabbed the broom and started swinging it and yelling at him, "Where have you been?" The detectives were trying to calm her, but she kept on screaming with the broom still in her hand.

The funny part was, just like I had done with my bicycle, he was keeping the car a secret. We learned that keeping secrets from your parents is not the smart thing to do. It will eventually come back to haunt you!

Harry left his job at the local butcher shop and went to work for a well-known supermarket chain. He worked for them for a few years and became a meat manager. He would many times bring his paperwork home. I remember Mom yelling at him because he had all the bills scattered all over the floor while he was doing them. Mom would ask him, "Are you a butcher or a secretary?"

The church I attended had many different organizations. The first group I joined was called the Olympians. In fact, I even got my friend Louis involved. Then I got deeply involved with GOYA, which stood for Greek Orthodox Youth of America.

We had an advisor named Jerry who would help us on many issues. Even with his own family life, he would go way out of his way to guide us. After we had our club meeting, we would go to a diner for a late snack and play the jukebox. For a nickel, you could play your favorite song.

The club did many things to raise money. We came up with the idea of having a play, in Greek of course. We had a lot of talent in the group, like my cousin Athena who used her expertise to write the words and put the production together.

We called the play *Kavanpoula*; that is Cinderella the way we knew it. I was going to play the fairy godmother. We had fun rehearsing and putting the acts together. When we did the performance, we had the audiences rolling in the aisles. It went over so well that we did two performances.

A church group from Brooklyn invited us to their annual Halloween costume party. I decided to go all out. I loved scary things, so I decided to play the Frankenstein monster.

One of my friends had made me platform shoes, which gave me five inches more in height. I tried everything on and even scared myself.

I always enjoyed pulling jokes, so to have some fun with my family, I took my costume, and I stuffed it and then laid it on the bed. My brother Harry was my first victim. He walked into the bedroom, and as soon as he saw it, he yelled out. Mom came running to see what had happened. She even gave a slight scream. After Mom saw it, she started yelling at me. After that, I knew I had a winner.

We had to take the subway because none of us was old enough to drive. It was so funny when we took the subway. Let just say, I got a lot of attention.

When we came out of the subway, there were two teenage girls sitting on a storefront step. It happened to be a store that sold monuments for cemeteries. Like I said, I always enjoyed playing jokes, so what better time to have a little fun?

I sneaked up behind them and slowly walked forward with my hands raised, making strange sounds. I never saw two girls scream and jump as they did. Before I could even say, "Happy Halloween," they were long gone. When we arrived, no one recognized who I was at first. We all had a fabulous time, and I even won first prize.

One Sunday, after church services, Gregg and I met this fellow named Bill. He was a camera bug. Wherever we went, so did his camera. We got him involved with the social club, and we would go to a lot of dances. He was always taking pictures and the girls thought he was a freelance photographer; so because of that, we got to meet a lot of girls. The funny thing was he eventually started doing just that.

I decided to run for club president, and I won. After I became club president, I got an invitation to another church club. I told my mother I would be home early, but because of a snowstorm, I got home late.

When I got home, no sooner than I had the key in the lock, Tessie was shouting out, "Mike, is that you?" She was always one who could not sleep until all of us were safely home; that was her nature.

I grew almost five inches by the time I was in my senior year. I was not as tall as my brothers, but it was gratifying knowing I was not going to be the shortest guy in my senior class.

The girls from the neighborhood I grew up with—Anna and her sister Cythera, and Dementia and my cousin Athena—I would treat them just like sisters. Was that because I had two sisters? It was not until I was in my upper teens that I saw girls in a different way.

By sheer coincidence, I had met this pretty girl at the Fifth Avenue public library; we were both doing extra credit. I liked this girl's company, so I asked to see her again. One event led to another, and before we realized it, we became mutually attracted. We were seeing each other almost every Saturday night.

After we had dated a few months, she invited me to her cousin's birthday party. I was in for a whopping surprise that night. I had dated many different girls over the last year; some of them I dropped, and some dropped me.

When I met her cousin, I discovered she was one of the girls I had stopped seeing. At that moment, I was speechless. When she saw me, she blasted me right where I stood. When the smoke cleared, my new girlfriend said, "I cannot believe you would do something like that. I never want to see you ever again."

I still tried to explain, but my efforts fell on deaf ears. What were the odds this would ever happen?

I learned something that night: be careful how you end a relationship, because you never know when it will come back to haunt you.

In 1958, I went to Times Square to bring in the New Year for the first time. This was going to be an experience I would always remember. Mom had warned me about going.

For years, I had watched it on TV, but until you go and live the experience of the crowd, you cannot put it into words. I never saw so many wild, crazy people in my life before; there was one minute when I felt like a sardine in a can. The next time I would see Times Square on New Year's Eve would be on television. The first lowering of the ball tradition started in 1907.

As we were growing up, we would celebrate each New Year's Eve with pots and pans. Mom would give us a pot and a spoon, and we would all run into the hallway making a racket and welcoming the New Year.

Whenever we went to Times Square, we would stop at a place called Grants to enjoy a hot dog or a hamburger smothered in onions for fifteen cents. That old saying, "If it tastes too good, it is not good for you," was true, but then who cared?

My brother Jack had worked for different companies and was making tremendous bucks. His career was in the field of computers, and he was a natural. I do not know whom he took after, most probably no one. I remember he was working in the Empire State Building. He invited both Harry and me to his office. He showed us this computer; it was the size of a car. He was explaining its operation and said in the future, this same computer would be no bigger than a shoebox. He was so right, and now they are even smaller.

I started working in the church office on Sundays after services. My responsibility was to be sure the church collections for the day were safely put in the safe. I would answer the phone, and I also took care of any paperwork and all donation fees for weddings and christenings.

It was a lot of fun. I got to meet all the nervous grooms and brides and made sure everything went off on schedule. Almost every Sunday, there were weddings and baptisms, and I would stay until the last sacrament was completed.

The parish priest, Father Kazanas, and I became close. He would pull off his collar at the end of the day and make a few joking comments. He had a magnetic, speaking voice, which captured everybody's attention.

The church club was nationwide, and every year, they would hold a convention in different parts of the country. The year while I was president, they were to have it right there in New York City.

They asked me to take charge of the hospitality committee. I knew the city remarkably well, so it made things a lot easier and that much more fun.

It was my responsibility to get free and discount tickets to different events and some shows. I also went to the visitors' center so that I could gather more activities. I had met this Greek girl who worked at the center, and we became friends.

After each day's events, I would take some of the visitors sightseeing. I came to discover the best time to see the city was after midnight; it was like a different city. I met people from all over the country.

The following year, I was reelected club president. It just happened that the next national convention was in held in Dallas, Texas. I wanted to go, but the club treasury could not afford it.

I decided to ask the president of the church to see if they would pay the expenses. Most of my fellow club members told me, "Good luck."

I got to talk to the church president on the subject. I put my charm to work. I mentioned that it was vital to have the church represented. After all, we were "the Greek Cathedral."

Within minutes, he said, "You sold me. I will talk to the board of directors."

I kept my fingers crossed. The following week, I got the okay; all my fellow club members were surprised.

Mom, being so old-fashioned, felt I was too young to go so far by myself.

My brother Harry came to my rescue; he told Mom, "He is eighteen, and it is time to break the ice."

She at first did not take to his opinion. Then she said to me, "What about your job?"

I told her, "I'm taking my vacation time, so stop worrying."

Thanks to Harry, I was on my way to Dallas, Texas. This was my first time going away on my own. To make matters even more exciting, I was flying, and Mom worried about the whole episode. Mom, as usual, gave me her famous saying, *"Ta matia sou dekatesita"* (Have fourteen eyes) and make sure to call.

Since this was my first time flying, I had to admit I was a little nervous. We landed at Love Field, which was between Dallas and Fort Worth. I met a few people who were also attending the convention, so we shared a cab. Once I had checked in at the hotel and gotten settled, I made sure to call home.

On one of the nights, a few of us drove to Fort Worth for dinner. We took the Dallas/Fort Worth Expressway, which was a super, twelve-lane highway, something I had never seen before. We ate dinner at this restaurant called the Cattleman's. While we were eating, of course dinner was steak, we could literally hear the cattle in the background. We came to find out the slaughterhouse was right behind the restaurant. "Now how fresh is that?"

At the dinner dance, I was talking and joking with some local people I had met. Out of the corner of my eye, I spotted this girl who got my attention. I asked one of the guys if he knew the girl who was wearing that Texas outfit. He replied, "Yes," the first thing he said about her was, "She is not Greek."

I said, "I could care less." He teased me and said she loved the Greek culture and was too smart for me.

I said, "Introduce me."

He then introduced us. When she first said hello, I think I fell in love with her Texan accent. Her name was Gayle, and she was nothing like any girl I knew back home.

We truly hit it off. We danced and chatted the entire night. I told her I would be leaving on Sunday, and I would love to see her again. I told her I had no car to get around. She said, "Be ready and in front of the hotel at 8:00 a.m. sharp. Do not eat breakfast."

I was up early. I was a little apprehensive, not knowing what to expect. She was like clockwork; she pulled up in this expensive convertible sports car and said, "Hop in."

While we were driving, she told me a little about herself. I was enjoying the scenery, and I even offered to drive. After a couple of hours, I asked where we were going. She stayed quiet for a moment and said, "You'll see."

She pulled up to this impressive, gigantic house. Again I asked where we were. She said, "We're at my parents' ranch."

I was speechless. I felt strange not knowing what to expect.

We walked into this immense foyer. It looked like a hotel lobby. The living room was bigger than my entire apartment back home. Her mother and younger sister greeted us, and we went to this outdoor garden terrace where we were going to have brunch.

We sat down, and their servant bought out all this food from eggs to steak. Her father, who towered a sturdy foot over me, came and joined us. He welcomed me with a really firm handshake. He looked like a real cowboy. All he needed was a six-shooter and a holster.

Then her father asked me all kinds of questions, like what part of the city did I live in and if I was attending school. I told him that I had just graduated.

He asked which college I attended. I immediately said, "No, I graduated high school."

He laughed. He said, "Make sure to show Mike some of the sights." He also asked me if I could ride a horse. I said I never had. He said this was an opportune time to learn.

After brunch, Gayle took me to the stable that looked more like a house from the outside. She told me to select a horse. I told her to choose one and please make sure he was a slow one. She saddled the horses. I felt useless because I did not know where even to start.

I slowly got on the horse. The horse must have sensed my fear and gave me a jerk forward. She yelled, and he settled down. Once I got myself in the saddle and got comfortable, we started out really slowly, and then, as they say in Texas, "we hit the trail."

I was getting more comfortable as we were riding. We must have ridden for a pleasant half hour. I asked how far this ranch went. She answered, "As far as you can see."

When I got off the horse, I was one large sore, especially where I had sat. She said to me that I was a natural, and I could fool anybody. We went back to have a tall, Texan-style iced tea to chill off.

We went to the other side of the ranch, and all I saw were oil wells—and I do not mean one or two. There were dozens, and they were all pumping oil. We then drove to a town called Johnson City where we had lunch. Again, I saw oil wells right smack in the middle of town. In the city, oil wells were something you did not see; there were only oil refineries in New Jersey.

She took me to a real, authentic Mexican restaurant. For the first time, I tasted a hot chili that would knock your socks off. From that day, I got hooked on chili. Later, we drove to where one of her dad's friends, a senator, lived. He lived on this immense hundred-acre ranch. Little did I know he would be the president someday.

After showing me sights, we headed back. I will never forget we went back to her parents' ranch where they were hosting an enormous barbecue. I had never seen so many cowboys and cowgirls in one domicile at one time, except maybe in the movies. I also had never seen (except maybe in a butcher shop) or eaten so much steak before that day.

We went riding again before it got dark. Later, I saw a sight that was one I will always remember. The stars were so vast and bright it was as if I could just reach out and grab one.

I had to get back, as much as I was enjoying myself. I had an early flight, and it was a long ride back to the hotel. She drove me back just before midnight. A few of my friends at the hotel were concerned. I assured them I had been in trustworthy hands.

This had to be one of the nicest times that I could remember. She wanted to come to New York for a visit. Now that I had met this lovely girl, I looked forward to seeing her again.

Well, it was back to the real world. Now I knew why they said everything was big in Texas. I told my family about my trip and how much I enjoyed my stay in Dallas and the other parts of Texas. Then I went on about all the friends I had made and especially the cowgirl I had met.

The first thing Mom asked was, "Is she Greek?"

I said, "No." I told them everybody would meet her one day when she came for a visit. Mom gave me a grin, as only a mother could.

The girl I had met in the visitors' center called me to invite me to a family birthday party at the Waldorf Astoria Hotel. I was thinking that was too ritzy for me. She was going with her parents, so I was going to meet her there.

It was a vigorous, healthy walk from my house. To play it safe, I did not tell my mother anything. I met her at the lobby, and we went into the party together. I got to meet her parents.

The party was for her uncle, who, to my surprise, was a well-known millionaire shipowner. A short time later, she introduced me to him; I was quite taken aback. He was not what I expected. He gave a sloppy appearance and had a nasty way about him. I learned something new that day: even as wealthy as he was, he was no better than the rest of us.

I could not get comfortable. Maybe it was the class of people; I just could not fit in with the crowd. I dated her a few times, but things did not turn out, so I stopped seeing her. This was one time I was glad I never told my mother.

Mom was taking a long, well-deserved trip back to Greece. This was her first trip back since she came to America. It was going to feel different, and as much as I loved her and would miss her, a short absence would be welcome.

Over the years, Mom always sent clothing to Greece whenever we outgrew it or just stopped wearing it. Now that she was going, she took a bunch of clothing back with her. Being she was going by steamship, there were no weight concerns. Mom did not mess around; she even purchased a new trunk just for that purpose.

We had to watch our sisters now that Mom was going to be gone for most of the summer. Between my brothers and me, how bad could it be? Well, let me just say, it was a nightmare, in more ways than you could imagine. My brother Jack said it would be a miracle if Mary survived until Mom got back.

Harry and I wanted to surprise Mom by redoing the kitchen. We all felt she deserved it because she was constantly trying to keep it clean and she just about lived in it.

While Mom was away, we were also invited for a Sunday dinner at Harry's future in-laws. I could not get over all the delicious food they prepared, starting with appetizers and all different types of pasta. Then after we had all finished those, they brought out the main course from meat to potatoes. I was totally shocked; I could not believe all the food for one sitting. I learned a whopping lesson that day: eat with your stomach and not your eyes. The trouble is do we ever really learn?

When Mom returned, we would all never forget how excited she was to be home. When she saw the kitchen, the way she reacted, it was worth every minute of the time we had spent on it. At least now she did not have to worry about painting this part of the apartment.

Weeks after she got back from her trip, our cousin sent her pictures that they took while she was there. We will never forget Jack's expression when he noticed one of the pictures. It seems that one of the cousins was wearing a suit that resembled his.

Jack was a sharp dresser; he only bought from the better men's shops, like Wallace. This was a summer suit, so when the summer was over, he would put it away until the following year. Mom thought that because he had not been wearing it all these months he did not want it anymore.

His search was now over. We all teased him about it because the cousin was the local postman in Mom's hometown in Greece.

Jack was a character in his own personal way. He told us different stories. Each was always better than the last. He always got a seat on the bus or subway, no matter how crowded it was. We would ask him what his secret was; his answer was a clear case of gas.

Our first cousin with the same name as Jack had won the Harvest Moon Ball dance back in the mid-fifties. Many people would think it was my brother Jack. He could easily get away with it, because he was a terrific dancer.

Jack was working for a company called Hertz as an executive VP, making substantial bucks. When the economy was on the downslide in the seventies, a lot of companies were letting the high-paid executives out of their contracts. He was no exception; their way of thinking was they could hire two younger fresh recruits just out of school for the money they were paying Jack.

Jack always seemed to bounce back. I guess it was in his blood. A short time later, through some contacts, he had hit it solid again with a company called Members Only. Jack, in a year, took the company from the red and put them in the black, with his computer expertise and his executive knowledge.

One of my high school friends, with whom I stayed in contact with after we graduated, asked me to do him a tremendous favor. It seems he had seen this girl on the subway and had fallen for her but was too embarrassed to introduce himself. He said to me, "I see how easy you get to meet people, especially girls." He wanted me to get involved by meeting her first and getting to know her and then introducing him.

He begged me. I said, "Are you crazy?"

"Please do this, and I will never ask another favor again."

I was thinking to myself, *How did I get myself involved with all this?* Being a softy, I said, "All right."

I met him where he saw her on the subway, and he gave me all the details. I told him it must be my way, with no expectation, and he agreed. While we were talking, he pointed her out. I said, "With her looks and figure, I doubt she is not seeing someone or even involved. I cannot guarantee positive results."

The following morning, I got all dolled up, and my mother asked where I was going so early and all dressed up. She asked, "Is this all about a girl?"

I said, "No. Where did you get that crazy notion?" I made up a story and quietly left.

I got to the subway station a few minutes earlier just to be sure I did not miss her. It was lucky I did because I spotted the girl going up the stairs. I was waiting for an opportune moment to make my move.

All of a sudden, this fellow greeted her with a kiss, and they walked off together. I was thinking to myself, *It looks like my friend is out of luck.* But I had come this far, so I continued the venture.

I followed them, and they went into a coffee shop (chock-full of nuts). I kept my distance after they got their coffee, and I got mine. I sat far enough away not to be obvious but close enough to hear them. I came to realize they were brother and sister.

My friend was still in luck. After a short time, he left. She was sitting there drinking the coffee. It was now time to make my move.

I walked past her table, and I purposely spilled my coffee on the table. I immediately apologized. Then I said, "Is everything all right? Did I burn you? Please, let me at least pay for any cleaning for your pretty coat."

She said, "Please do not worry," but I insisted. As I was talking to her, I was cleaning up the mess I had made.

She said, "I will be late for work. I have to go."

I said, "May I walk with you?"

She hesitated and then replied, "If you wish." I introduced myself, and she told me her name. We continued walking to her place of employment. We chatted about things in general, and I was thinking to myself, *This girl is much too pretty not to be involved.* When we got to where she worked, which happened to be Bloomingdale's, I told her my mother loved to shop at the store and so did I.

I asked, "May I see you again, so that I can pay for the cleaning of your coat?"

She said, "Do not worry about it," but she gave me her phone number just the same.

My friend called me to see what was going on, so I told him I got her phone number. He said, "Swell, what is it?"

I said, "One just cannot call like that. Let me get to know her a little better."

I called her a few times and just chatted, but I did not make a date just yet. My friend would call me constantly. He was being extremely demanding. He said I was taking too long and he did not like the way I was handling the situation. Then he started being terribly pushy; he insisted on me giving him her phone number. I said a flat "no." I reminded him of our agreement.

My mother, with her Greek radar, heard me arguing and said, "Is this about a girl?" She started shouting at me and said, "Don't get involved."

I was not getting anywhere with him. I told him, "No," again. I was furious. I just hung up. Now I was sorry I had ever gotten involved.

I carefully thought it out and decided not to get any more involved. So I decided to end it on both ends. He became more like an enemy than a friend after all this. He thought that I was seeing her secretly.

Another lesson in life: never get between a friend and a girl.

A lot of my other friends were moving or had moved from the neighborhood as we were growing up. I stayed in touch with my friend Louis, but like everything else, one thing leads to another. One thing I did learn was if you do not stay on top of keeping in touch with people, they just disappear.

Chapter 10

New Lessons in Life

My brother Harry, now that he had his own car registered under his own name, started giving me driving lessons. The car he purchased was a 1949 Chevy convertible. It was a stick shift. It had Cadillac-style fins, fender skirts, and Buick air vents with leopard-print seat covers. He loved this car, as much as a friend.

Living in the city, you could literally see the soot that came out of the

Harry and his car

smokestacks from the electric power plant (Con Edison). The soot would settle on everything. Because of that, Harry was constantly washing his car. Many times, I would help him as a payback for his driving lessons.

The biggest problem was it was a stick shift, and I could not get comfortable. No matter how hard he tried to show me, I just could not get the feel of it. I was not sure which was louder: the gears when I was shifting or Harry's teeth grinding. So after a few lessons and after almost running down some pedestrians, I decided to go to a driving school.

Most cars were stick shift. Automatic was a new feature on newer cars. Turn signals were using your hand to tell others you were turning. Automatic turn signals were just being introduced into newer cars, so unless you had a new car, you had to use your hands to signal.

Signaling was most beneficial to convey respect to other drivers whenever one made a turn or a sudden stop. Today, all cars have them, but it seems so many do not know that their cars have them. If you do not believe me, just take notice.

I applied at a driving school to have them teach me on an automatic. Once I had my license, I could then learn to drive a stick. After many weeks of lessons, I felt I was ready.

The morning of the test, the instructor picked me up in this large car. I was quite upset because I had been practicing on this smaller car, and now I had this tank to drive. I asked the instructor where the other car was; he told me that someone had had an accident with it, and it was in the repair shop—just my luck. I only had a few minutes to get the feel of this tank; it was now or never.

When I completed the road test, the examiner handed me a slip and said, "Better luck next time." I'd failed because I tapped another car's bumper while parking.

All I could do now was reschedule my test. I wanted the same car that I had originally been instructed to drive. When I completed my road test the second time, I passed with a perfect score.

Now that I had my license, it felt fantastic, but unfortunately, I was not going to have a car just yet, because of the price of the car and insurance.

I would practice on Harry's car, and he would yell at me every time I did not shift properly. I still could not feel comfortable, so I just gave up for the time being.

Another lesson: to keep the peace, it is wisely suggested not to let any family member teach another to drive!

A distant cousin had just recently opened a bakery shop in Astoria, Queens. He had a problem finding reliable help. That sounds familiar. He had asked our mother to work a few hours to help. Mom was never one to say no.

Harry and I would sometimes pick her up from work when he was off. We both had the same habit. We would treat ourselves to these pistachio nuts that they sold out of this large jar. Mom would yell at us and say, "*Thro-pea!*" (Shame on you!)

After a while, her part-time hours got to be more like full-time. She would leave the house before 7:00 a.m. and not get home till after 4:00 p.m., and then she had to start making supper.

Mom would enjoy her after-work boost. She would on occasion have a shot of Scotch or whatever was available. After a while, she would complain about feeling tired and having a few aches and pains. We told her maybe this work was not for her.

This one day, Harry and I went to pick her up. We got there early, so we surprised her. We saw her and another woman doing a job that I never in my life do. They were folding and cutting these thin sheets of dough (fillo). They were both as white as snowmen, covered in flour from their heads to their shoes.

After watching them both working, we were surprised at the amount of labor and standing they had to endure. Now we could see the reason she would come home feeling so tired. We told her again to quit. She went on and said he could not find reliable help. No matter how much she would complain about her aches, she would continue to work.

Harry, on occasion, would get tickets to the Jets games, when they played at Shea Stadium. The first time he took me, it had to be below 0. No matter what I did, I just could not warm up. Maybe one had to be a die-hard fan to cope with that freezing temperature. The next time I would see the Jets playing was on TV.

I met this girl who was part Greek. I guess this made Mom half happy. She was a ballerina.

I got to meet her two bosses. They were both extremely friendly, and gay—not that there is anything wrong with that. We became friends; I enjoyed their company, and they enjoyed mine.

Not having a car, I had no choice but to use mass transit, so I always took the subway whenever I went to see her. One Saturday night, well past midnight, I had just dropped her off from a party we had attended earlier.

I was standing at the end of the platform waiting for the train. It was unusually quiet for a Saturday night. I had just recently purchased a brand-new camera, which I was holding.

Two guys about my age and size slowly started walking toward me. One walked past me. The other stopped on the other side and said, "Neat camera. I want it."

I said, "I do not think so."

He pulled out a switchblade and again said, "I want the camera."

Stupid me, I was thinking to myself, *I paid a lot of money for this camera.* I was not going to just give it to these punks. So I yelled out, "If you want it, come and get it." The one guy must have chickened out, because he left. I took off my jacket and put it around my arm. Then, I shouted out, "Okay, smart guy, now what?"

He came at me, and I moved to the side with the jacket still wrapped around my arm. Our arms were interlocked, and I was trying to force the knife out of his hand. He came down with the knife; it went right into his thigh. He gave a shout, and he then started running off with the knife still in him. I started yelling and cursing him.

By the time, the police arrived, they were far gone; they searched the vicinity, but they managed to get lost. The police officer filled out an incident report, and I gave him all the details.

I never realized, with all the commotion, that the knife had slashed my left hand, and I was bleeding. With my handkerchief, I put direct pressure on the wound until I got some medical attention. When the medics came, they just bandaged me up. I told them I would prefer to see my own doctor if needed.

I knew I could wash the blood off my hands, but the bandage, that was a different story. Sunday morning, Mom saw my hand. She went on, "Now how did you do that?" I told her I had just cut my hand by accident. While she was doing the sign of the cross, she said I had better go to the hospital and have it checked out.

A few days later, that same police officer called me to see how I was. Thank God I answered the phone. He told me they never found anyone that matched their descriptions, but he reassured me guys like that soon had their day.

After that, whenever I took the subway, I made it a point to make sure I remained among the crowds. I was not taking any more chances on something like that happening again. I also kept anything I felt was of any real value out of sight.

I knew why they said, "Out of sight, out of mind." I had told no one the true story about that. The knife wound left me with a scar that I still carry.

My girlfriend's bosses were hosting a Christmas pageant and a party to follow. She introduced me to a few of her friends. One of her friends told me that he was dating her. I was somewhat disillusioned, mostly because she had told me she was not dating or seeing anyone. Later, when I questioned her, she told me that they were just close friends. At this point, I did not know who to believe.

Her bosses gave a New Year's party; we all had a few drinks, maybe one too many. Come midnight, we all came together and brought in the New Year.

A few weeks later, I invited her and a few of her friends, whom I had met at the New Year's party, to my house. Everybody was out of the house for one reason or another.

Her alleged unannounced boyfriend said to me privately, "How about a kiss?"

I quickly shoved him off and said out loud, "Are you crazy? I'm not that type."

He said I gave him a hug and kiss on New Year's Eve. I loudly replied, "It was New Year's, and I was just being friendly to all."

He apologized and said to the others, "Let's go." I told her that I would take them home. Two of them said they were going someplace, and they left.

I did something I would regret. With the weather being exceptionally mild for this time of the year, I asked one of the brothers from the restaurant if I could borrow his car, which happened to be a convertible. Without a second thought, he gave me the keys and said, "Be careful."

She asked, "Where did you get this car?"

I told her it was a friend's, and I'd just borrowed it for the first time.

She sat in the front, and he sat in the back. I pulled out, and this speeding car cut me off. As I was turning sharply to avoid the oncoming car, I swerved to the left, hitting a parked truck. I totally demolished the front of the car, and both of them went flying forward. She hit her knee on the dashboard, and he hit his head on the front seat. As for me, I was all right. I made sure they were both okay. I now had to tell my friend about the accident.

I felt terrible about what happened because he always had babied this car. When he saw the car, I could sense his feelings. He called the police to file an accident report. I explained what happened, but the car that caused the accident was long gone. I told the police that it all happened so fast I was not able to get the license plate number.

I told my friend I would pay the deductible; he said not to worry about it. If there was one thing my father taught us, it was to take responsibility seriously. I gave him some of the money I was saving for my car. I learned a whopping, expensive lesson that day; when one takes responsibility, one must be prepared.

Because of the accident, my girlfriend was not able dance for a few weeks. As for her friend, he just had a slight bump on his head. Now I can see how seat belts could have helped with this accident. Unfortunately, seat belts were not available then.

If I had been a more experienced driver, I might have avoided the accident. I got to realize that every day is a new life experience.

A short time later, I told her that our mutual friend was "gay." She said, "I do not believe it." Then she asked, "Would you stoop that low? Are you that jealous? I've known him for years, and he never gave me any evidence of being gay."

Out loud, I said, "Well, he is. He tried to kiss me that day at my house."

She went on and said, "I do not believe it. And I never want to see you again."

I said, "Fine. If you are that naive, I feel the same way."

I left her with the comment, "I do not care that he is gay. It is his life to live. I have nothing against that, but when they push themselves on me, that changes everything. Your bosses are gay, and it does not bother me. They respect that I am heterosexual." I gave her wish and ended it.

My friends from the restaurant asked me to do them a tremendous favor. They had another restaurant in Harlem that they wanted to sell. With business being so poor, it made it more difficult.

Their goal was for me to go and buy a lot of items, like sandwiches and even meals. Once a week, they would give me one hundred dollars, and sometimes even more to spend, so it would increase sales, which were lacking. I would bring some meals home, and Mom would question me. Then she called me "*vlocker*" (stupid) for getting involved with other people's problems. I would give most all the food to the homeless. How much could I eat? It must have been successful, because after a few months, they managed to sell it. I also learned why they were called "greasy spoons."

My friend Gayle from Texas was planning to spend a long weekend in New York. This was going to be her first trip to New York City. I told my mother about her visit. I could see she was not too pleased. Mom said, "What about your job and your job at the church?"

I told her, "I took care of everything. Stop worrying."

I gave her a full tour of the city, starting with a boat ride around Manhattan Island; then we went to the Statue of Liberty and to the Empire State Building and finished up at the United Nations. One nifty thing about living right in the heart of the city is we did not need a car to get around.

Saturday, I took her to Central Park where we spent the day, and then we went to an early movie. She suggested that we should go the 21 Club. I was somewhat thrown by this, mainly because it was more than I could afford.

She said, "My dad told me the restaurant is exceedingly expensive. It was his suggestion. In fact, he said that he would pick up the tab."

I said, "No, you are my guest, but thank him just the same."

We went upstairs to this intimate room, where we were treated like royalty; it had a really warm, cozy glow that created an enchanting and unforgettable evening.

When the waiter brought the check, she insisted on paying it. I said again, "Thanks, but you are my guest, and it is my turn to express my hospitality." So I tapped some money from my car account. I had waited this long. What was a few months' more going to matter?

Before I had left Saturday morning, Mom said, "Be sure to bring her for dinner Sunday." It was gratifying to hear her say this. When I told her about coming for Sunday dinner, she gave me a loving hug.

Everybody gave her a warm welcome, which got to her. She had a shopping bag with a cake and a bottle of wine. As we were eating, she was overwhelmed with all the different Greek dishes Mom had made. Mom went overboard just a little more, and of course, she would never admit it, but that was Mom!

The following day, she phoned me and said she had had a terrific time and was glad she came. Everybody liked her, especially her Texan way of speaking. Mom was being polite about it all, but I could sense that because she was not Greek, she would not talk much about it.

While working in the church office, I was coming down the stairs just after a wedding was finishing up, and this girl asked me where the restroom was. The same girl came into the office asking how to get back to the church. We started talking; one thought led to another, and before I knew it, I had her phone number. She worked for a doctor, and the best part was the office was just a few blocks from where I lived.

One day, while I was visiting her at the office, she introduced me to her boss, the doctor. We chatted like old friends, and he invited us to his summerhouse for a Saturday barbecue.

She picked me up, and I drove to his summer getaway up in Monroe, New York. This was where the weird part began. I found the house almost like I knew exactly where it was. When we walked into the house, a chill went through me. Her boss and his wife greeted us, and then his wife gave us a tour of the house. As she was showing us, I knew the layout exactly. It was a weird feeling, and something I could not explain.

After we ate, I said, "Let's play some tennis."

She asked, "How do you know that we have a tennis court?"

Well, it turns out they had one, and I knew exactly where it was. When my girlfriend realized they had a tennis court, she freaked out, because she did not even know.

She was getting a little concerned and apprehensive. She said that it seemed as though I had been here before. I told her it was a strange feeling that I could not explain. Everybody was taken aback by the fact I knew a lot about the house and its surroundings, especially since this was my first time here ever.

While we were playing tennis, that same chilling feeling went through me, and I told her it felt as if I had played there before. Again, I could not explain this bizarre feeling.

While we were driving home, my friend was not particularly talkative. I could see she was bewildered by this. After this, she started giving me the cold shoulder. She started avoiding my phone calls. She was always making excuses. After a while, I read the handwriting on the wall and stopped calling her.

On some warm nights, I would take my dates to a drive-in movie. Afterward, we would go to Jones Beach to watch the submarine racers.

My mother would tease me by saying I was going out with more girls than I had hairs on my head. (That was when I had some hair.)

Mom would say I should find a lovely Greek girl and settle down. I would come back with a sly comment and say, "I could not find one."

She would get mad at me for making that kind of remark. I told her when Miss Right came along, she would be the first to know.

I had a bad habit of always taking a catnap before going on a date. There were times I would oversleep, and Mom had to wake me. Sometimes, I would doze off when I was at a girl's house while we were watching TV. Was this a Pappas curse?

With all the non-Greek girls I was dating, one of my friends wanted to set me up with a blind date who happened to be Greek. He told me that her family was financially well off. At first, I was against the idea, but he talked me into doing it. He said I had nothing to lose, and besides, I would make my mother happy.

So he set the date up, and my mother was overjoyed, because she knew something about the girl's family. I reminded him I had no car, and that was going to cause a slight problem. He said, "Don't worry about it; she has one, and she would be more than happy to pick you up."

Even though, I had had girls driving me in the past, I always felt kind of funny, especially now going on a blind date. What would her family think? Somehow, Mom found out she was picking me up and got mad. She said, "Gentlemen do not allow girls to pick them up."

So I did not say anything more about it. In fact, I planned to meet her at another location.

She drove up in this brand-new Cadillac, which got my attention. She got out of the car and introduced herself. She handed me the car keys. I was thinking to myself that she had a pretty shape, was not bad looking, and drove a superb car. Plus, her family was loaded. How bad was that?

As we were driving, I noticed she kept looking into her handbag. We seemed to be hitting it off, and we decided to take in a movie.

She wanted to go see a movie called *Gigi*, which I was not too thrilled about. But being a gentleman, I bit my tongue and said, "Okay." Before going to the seats, we got some snacks. Then she wanted to sit close to the screen and away from the crowd. I was not too thrilled, but again, I bit my tongue. While we were watching the movie, she was constantly looking into her handbag.

At one point, I heard her whispering. Then, all of a sudden, this little head stuck up out of her handbag. I had to take a double look. I was trying to keep my voice down, and I said, "What the heck is that?"

She quietly said, "It is my dog, Cleo. She is a miniature Chihuahua; she goes wherever I go. I never leave her behind."

I had seen a lot of strange things, but this had to be the best.

I was planning on a snack after the movie, but after this, I decided not to bother. In fact, this was my first and last date with her. I said, "Money or no money, this is not for me."

She dropped me off, gave me a kiss on my cheek, and said, "I hope to see you again soon."

My friend called me the next day to ask me how it went. I said to my friend, "Thanks for nothing." I did not go into detail. He was sorry it did not work out. My mother even got mad at me because I did not give it a chance. Was I being too quick to judge?

I would meet a lot of Greek girls at the Manhattan Center dances, but many times, I would strike out or never followed through. This one time, I saw this girl who caught my attention, as well as others'. She was beautiful and had a shape that looked like a model. I managed to get to dance with her. Everything was going swell. I thought I had found a Greek goddess—until she started talking. It was like my balloon busted. Not even five minutes passed before I just said, "I'm going to the men's room," and never returned. Another lesson: do not judge a girl by the way she might look.

The same night, shortly thereafter, I got lucky and met this girl. We hit it off. I took her phone number and made a date with her. She had come with some other girls, and because I had no car, she went home with them.

It was not until later that I realized where she lived. It was way out on the Brooklyn/Queens border in a section called Myrtle Avenue. I got to find out it was almost an hour journey by subway each way. I was not looking forward to that, but until I got a car, I had no other choice. I knew Mom would be delighted, so I told her I had met a girl, and she was all Greek. Again, she was thrilled that I was seeing a Greek girl.

She invited me to a Sunday dinner that she said she was going to prepare. Mom always told us it was essential whenever we were invited to someone's home to never go empty-handed. In fact, she went as far as to buy a cake for the occasion. This was just typical of Mom.

She cooked me an authentic Greek meal from *"mezedes"* (appetizers) to dessert. There were a few dishes I was not too thrilled to see. While growing up, there were many meals my mother made that I did not eat. One particular dish was named *"bamyies"* (okra). At first, I was a little hesitant to eat it. Call me silly for never trying it at home, but so as not to hurt her feelings, I tried hers.

I took a small piece, and I truly loved it. I learned something from this: I was letting my eyes do my tasting. After this, my eating habits made a total about-face. When I told my mother, she started laughing. She said, "Who is this girl who got you to try something I have been trying to make you eat all these years?" Mom wanted to meet her. I told Mom to relax. I was just getting to know her.

We dated a few months; the problem was she wanted a commitment. I was not ready to get involved just yet, so I ended it. When I stopped seeing her, my mother got terribly upset.

I told my mother, "If you get upset and angry every time I stop seeing Greek girls, I just will not bother saying anything anymore. She scolded me again for talking out of line.

My new motto was, "I do not tell her anything, and if I do, no more than I have to."

It was a slow process saving for my car with all these unexpected expenses that I was encountering. I was extremely fortunate because most of the girls I dated had their own cars, so I was able to take advantage of it.

Does this mean that I was a gigolo? Because this rumor got started. I had a fair idea of who might have started it, but at that point, I did not care. I never let any girl I dated pay her way, much less mine.

I started working in a electronic testing laboratory shortly after I graduated high school. The hours were from 3:00 p.m. to 11:30 p.m. weekdays. If I worked on Saturday, it was only a half of a day. Just like Harry did, I helped with some of the bills.

I would take the bus or sometimes the subway. No matter what time it was, Mom always had supper waiting for me.

I decided to open a checking account. Again, this was all new to me. A few weeks after I opened my checking account, I received a credit card. What got my attention was that I could draw up to five hundred dollars with no credit check. The funny part was I had never asked to receive it.

I decided to take advantage of it. I told the bank teller, "I'd love to take the maximum amount of money on this offer." The teller never even asked me for any identification, just my signature. Before I realized it, she handed me all these bills. I thought I had hit the jackpot.

I received a statement from the bank for the money I received. I was thinking to myself, *I have to pay it back with interest, but I never asked for it.* I told my brothers about it and asked them if I had to pay it back, and they both laughed. They both told me nothing was free in this world.

I had spent some of the money, and I was going to use the rest to buy my car. I refused to pay the interest, so I returned the money I still had. I could have beaten the system if I had had someone else withdraw the money. I guess I was just too stupid or just too honest.

It was not until years later that they found out they were losing thousands of dollars by just giving open credit to anyone, without any thought of a credit check.

This sounds so familiar; I always wonder what kinds of people (CEOs) run the financial and large corporations. I also wonder about the politicians then and now. I guess we never learn because history just repeats itself. Another lesson in life, but do they ever learn?

Some days, while I was going to work, this high school girl would get on the bus after she got out of school. We would both get off at the same bus stop. She apparently lived on the same block that I worked on. This went on for a few weeks. She never spoke to me, but I could sense she was checking me over.

Harry got engaged to his girlfriend Lillian, who was from the neighborhood. Her family gave them an engagement party, to which they invited family and friends.

While I was talking with Harry, someone put her hands over my eyes and then said, "Guess who."

I turned around and said, "You seem mighty familiar." After a few seconds, I realized who she was, and I was totally taken by surprise. It was that same girl from the bus. She looked totally different; she was dressed in this sexy outfit and looked a lot older. I said, "What brings you here?"

She said, "My mother and your brother's future mother-in-law happen to be best friends."

She saw a picture of my brother and me. When she saw me on the bus, she was not sure if we were the same. She said, "I apologize if I made you feel uncomfortable while we were on the bus."

I had to admit she was an exceptionally pretty and sexy-looking girl but definitely too young for me. We became talking friends, but she wanted to be more than that. My mistake was telling her she was too young.

She kept on insisting that she was mature for her age. She would most of the time meet me on the bus and make conversation. Not to be rude, I would just listen, which made matters worse.

When I had finally saved enough money, I started seriously looking for a car. After looking at different cars, my pick was a 1955, two-door, hardtop Oldsmobile. The only downside was the car did not have power steering. To make money matters even worse, because of a previous accident, my insurance premium was almost twice what it would have been.

I learned to budget myself, because I knew it was going to be a struggle. Now that I had a car, I was up against another obstacle: parking.

Not having any power steering, let me say, parallel parking was no joke, especially in tight spots. I bought curb feelers for parking, so I could hear them rubbing the curb to know how close I was.

Then I had to make sure I moved the car before a certain time or risk the possibility of getting a parking ticket or maybe even being towed.

I never parked in the same spot, but not because I did not want to. There were times I had to park far away from my house, just to find a spot. There were a few times I even forgot exactly where I did park it and literally had to go hunting for it.

One morning, I overslept, but thanks to Mom's awareness, she woke me. She was yelling, "Your car is getting towed!" I dressed so quickly. Talk about timing. I would have been out of luck if I had taken a few seconds longer.

Harry had gotten his share of parking tickets over the years. We had some friends who would get parking tickets as if they were giving them as gifts. If I would get one, it would bother me. I did not want to give away my money unnecessarily.

Now that I had a car, I started driving to work. Doing this, I would avoid running into the young girl. So I figured the less she saw me, the more likely she would be to forget me. Boy was I wrong. She would wait by the lobby.

My friends at work would tease me and make remarks about stealing the baby carriage and that she was jailbait. I remained her friend hoping she would get tired of me. That was not going to happen, so I had to consider other measures to end it. It took a while, but over time, I finally was able to free myself from her.

A few of us who drove to work made a deal with one of the parking garages to park, because parking at work was also a problem. Little did I know whose spot I was occupying.

Once a month, we worked a half day on Saturday, so we parked in the same spots. The first Saturday I worked, as I was leaving to go home, I saw a note on my windshield. The message read, "You are parking in my spot, so stop parking here."

As I was throwing the note into the trash basket, this older gentleman shouted out, "That's me left you the note!" I was thinking to myself, *Who is this idiot?* Because he looked awfully familiar. He started yelling at me and even threatened me for parking in his spot.

I started to apologize, and he went on like a lunatic yelling. He said, "Do you know who I am?

I said, "Should I?"

He replied, "I'm Walter Cronkite."

I replied, "For someone of your status, you are a particularly nasty individual."

As I was leaving, he said, "I will talk to management and make sure you do not park here anymore."

It is sometimes surprising to see how people truly are. When I saw him on TV, he always gave such a positive appearance. Now that I had seen him in person, he was so different. Did I bring out his dark side? I continued to park in the same garage; I just stayed far away from his parking spot.

While I was club president, I got involved with finding a location for the local convention at the Catskill Mountains. Not everybody had a car, so I volunteered to drive. Mom would yell at me for being too kindhearted, but that was me. While driving down the mountainside, being a new driver, I never gave braking a second thought; I kept on riding the brakes.

While we were all talking, we came across a detour, and I realized I had no brakes. Everyone became quiet; at first, I did not want to alarm everyone. I had no choice but to tell them. One of the girls screamed, and another one fainted. I kept my calm and was able to keep the car on the road, even around the curves passing up other cars. God had to be watching over us; all of a sudden, we came to a hilly part, which managed to slow the car, I was able to use the emergency brake.

We pulled into this gas station to have the brakes checked. The attended told me just to wait a while until the brakes cooled down. Plus, it gave us time to settle our nerves.

Harry made the decisive move and married his neighborhood sweetheart Lillian. They had a lovely Greek/Italian wedding that I will always remember. It was good to see Mom wear a dress that was a color other than black, which she hadn't done since Dad passed away.

My friend Louis and I both enjoyed taking movies. Since I was in the bridal party, he took movies of the wedding, using these bright spotlights that were blinding everybody.

Now with Harry out of the house, I felt outnumbered with no other male living in the same house. It was going to feel strange without him around every day.

Shortly after he had gotten married, he received his notice (greetings) from Uncle Sam; he never even opened it. Without thinking twice, he went to an induction center in Brooklyn and joined the army reserves.

Mom was a worrier, and this just added one more thing to her agenda. Even though he was married, Mom would worry. "When you are all parents, then and only then will you understand."

My first year I was working, I got two weeks' vacation, so I decided to take some day trips to the beach. My second week, I went out to the church camp, which had reopened out on Long Island in a town called Yaphank. I spent a few days relaxing and helping some of the camp counselors.

I went into the town one afternoon to get a few things that the director needed. After I had everything, I started heading back. I started to turn onto this main road, when all of a sudden, a beach ball came rolling out between two parked cars.

Not thinking twice, I immediately slammed on my brakes, and the car behind me hit my rear bumper. He started calling me rude names. Then, all of a sudden, out of nowhere, this toddler came after the ball. I quickly jumped out of the car.

The mother came after him. She was a nervous wreck but certainly grateful that no one had gotten hurt. She apologized for what had just happened. I told her, "Thank God nothing happened. Kids will be kids." The police came and saw everything was okay. I told the driver not to worry about it; there was no damage to be concerned about. Thank goodness for metal bumpers.

The moral of this is whenever you see a ball rolling, you can bet your life that a person, but must probably a child, will follow right behind it.

One afternoon, they were taking some of the children horseback riding, and they asked me to help chaperone. I looked forward to going horseback riding. It had been a while since I had been on one. I took some of the children in my car. When we got to the stables, they started assigning horses. There were about a dozen children ranging in age from about ten to twelve years old.

The stable man asked me if I had ridden a horse before.

I replied, "Like a cowboy."

As we were leaving, he said, "Just be careful. Your horse loves to run when he sees the open range."

My big mouth, just what I wanted to hear.

When we started out, I took up the rear of the group. We were on a trail moving relatively slowly. I was enjoying the ride when all of a sudden, I saw that just ahead, the trail opened up. I knew if I could see it, the horse could see it, too.

I was ready. No sooner than we got to the open range, as much as I tried to hold him back, he just took off like a speedy bullet. Everybody thought I was showing off, but I was definitely not. I finally got the horse to slow down and rejoin the group.

The children got a hefty kick out of it, and I got a new nickname after that; they called me "Speedy Mike." The few days with the kids were fun and relaxing. The night before I left, they had a cookout, and I told some scary stories by the campfire. The camp director thanked me and said I was welcome back anytime.

Ever go somewhere and forget where you parked? A few of my friends and I decided to go to Jones Beach. We left early to avoid the beach traffic. When we parked, no one even thought about or paid attention to where.

It started getting pretty crowded, so we decided to call it a day. On the way to the car, we met some girls and started making conversation. One thing led to another, and we decided to have something to eat. We walked along the beach looking for a place. After we ate, we decided to stay, so we hung out with the girls. A few hours later, I was getting pretty burned, so we all decided to call it a day. I lucked out and got a phone number of one of the girls.

With all the walking, we were not sure where we had parked. We walked back to where we thought the car was, but all we could see were hundred of cars and no sign of ours. We looked, but we could not find it. It was not until hours later when the parking lot was starting to empty that we saw it. The funny thing was, it was right where we had parked it.

After that, I knew why they had signs with letters or numbers in the parking lots; the fact is one must read them.

Mom told me that the husband of a daughter of her friend had just opened an auto repair shop. She said, "Why not take your car there for service? He is a young Greek fellow just starting out." So I decided to take a chance. I had been taking it to a local gas station for service, so I had nothing to lose—or did I?

He lived just around the corner, and his shop was in Long Island City, right across the Fifty-Ninth Street (Queensboro) Bridge. Over the months, we became somewhat friendly.

I would take the car there religiously, every one thousand miles or every three months for service, plus any other work the car required. So this went on for well over a year.

One day, while I was in Brooklyn to take care of something, I noticed that one rear tire was getting low on air. I was lucky that it happened right by an auto repair shop.

After I waited a short time, the serviceman, who was also the owner, jacked up the rear of the car to remove the tire. He said to me after he fixed the tire, "I want to check your front end."

He said, "Your front wheels do not look right." He went on and said, "Your front wheels are toeing in, which is not normal."

I said, "Okay." I had no inkling what he meant. He jacked up the front end and looked at it. He hesitated a second and then shouted, "Boy, are you an extremely lucky guy!" He said that if I had driven the car just a few more miles or hit a pothole, I would have definitely lost one of my front wheels, and maybe both.

I yelled out, "What?"

He said, "Someone up there is watching out for you." He asked, "Don't you service your car? When was the last time the car was greased?"

I replied, "Are you kidding? I just recently did, and every one thousand miles."

He said abruptly, "This car has not been greased properly for a long time." He showed me the front end, and I saw this ball joint that looked like someone's bald head.

My Greek temper was just about ready to boil over. What was this guy doing while he was taking my money? He apparently was not servicing the car.

I asked the man how much it was going to cost to repair. He said about seventy-five dollars. I told him I only had twenty dollars on me. The man was exceptionally meticulous about it. He said, "Anybody with this luck, I can trust." He said I could bring the difference or send it to him. I could not thank him enough for trusting me, and I assured him I would not disappoint him.

I told him I would like to have the two worn pieces that were replaced. The next day, I mailed him a check with a note thanking him. Then I paid my so-called friend, the mechanic, a visit. I did not usually get this mad, but my Greek temper was still boiling.

I had both pieces that the mechanic had given me. I took one of them and threw it through his front glass door. I then walked in, shouting at the top of my voice and cursing him out. I called him every nasty Greek word I could think of as I threw the other piece, almost hitting him.

He shouted, "You're crazy!"

I said, "Call me whatever, but what you did is a crime. I almost got killed because you never serviced my car as charged. How many people have you cheated by taking their money and not doing any service on their car? I will make sure others learn about this."

As I was walking out, I yelled, "If you call yourself a friend, then I do not need any enemies."

The woman's husband had told my mother before I had a chance to explain to her in detail what had happened. As soon as I walked into the house, Mom was shouting at me. She wanted to know why I broke the mechanic's window. I tried to explain what had occurred, but she did not want to listen. She told me to apologize for my actions. I refused to because I felt deep down I was right.

I later found out that my mother, being old-fashioned and never wanting to give the picture that we were evil people, gave him the money for the window that I broke.

When she told me this, my Greek temper was over its boiling point. I went straight to where he lived. I demanded he give the money back or else he would regret it. He started cussing me in Greek, and I told him he would regret he ever knew me.

Maybe I was being mean, but I wanted satisfaction. I asked a few of my friends at work for a few suggestions on how to get back at him. They gave me a few nifty ideas, and I was determined to follow up on one of them.

When I finally calmed down, I remembered what my father had told me, and I just swallowed my pride. It was just a matter of time. Sure enough, less than a year later, his business went south, and I was never more satisfied.

It was not just me he took for a ride. I became a powerful believer that the things one does in life will eventually come back twofold. The unfortunate part is it is difficult to determine where trust starts and ends; if you cannot trust so-called friends, whom can you trust?

I wanted to give the girl I had met at Jones Beach a call. The phone number had gotten smeared, and I could not see the last number clearly. Just my luck, and to make matters worse, I was not even sure of her name.

She was a terrific-looking girl, so I decided to take a chance. I called the number and just filled in the last number, which I could not read. I called almost every number with no luck. Then I tried the last number; it was this or nothing. A woman answered the phone. I said, "Hi, this is Mike. Remember? From Jones Beach?"

She said, "I think you want my daughter." A girl got on the phone, and it was she. I lucked out. We started chatting, and I made a date with her for the next Saturday night. She gave me her address and directions.

I told Mom I had a date for this Saturday night, and she asked if I had I forgotten about taking her to Theo (uncle) Mike's. I told her I could still do it, but I knew she was not too thrilled about it.

I dropped her off, and I stayed a few minutes. She asked, "What time are you planning on picking me up?"

I was thinking, How do I get out of this, if I can? I told her, "About midnight."

She said in Greek, "Are you for real? Tomorrow is Sunday; that is much too late."

My godmother heard all this and said, "I'll take her home."

I thanked her, and I was on my way.

While I was driving, I felt like a jerk because I had totally forgotten her name, so I had to make it a point get her name without looking like an idiot. When I got to her house, there was no answer. I was not late; in fact, I was a few minutes early. I was thinking to myself I had been stood up and at her house. I waited about a half hour and decided to leave and mark it up to a loss.

So I went back to pick up my mother. Everybody was surprised to see me. I was too embarrassed to tell them what had happened. I just told her that I had changed my mind.

I was reading in the newspaper a short time later that a girl fitting her description had been found murdered in her family's car. Her name sounded familiar, but I was still not quite sure. What got me was it happened just about the same time I was there. It certainly freaked me out. I never called that number again, wondering if it was the girl or not.

Some of the guys after work on payday started going to Germantown for some drinks. Every week, the guys kept on bugging me to go, so I gave in eventually and went.

I told Mom, "Do not wait supper for me. I am going out with my friends from work."

She said, "Do not get in any trouble."

I assured her I was not going to get in trouble and told her to stop worrying.

Just my luck, the first time I went with them, a fight broke out, and somehow I got into the middle of it. I was just minding my own business when this individual decided to take a swing at this other guy and hit me.

My friends saw this, and they all joined the ruckus. All hell broke out. I just kept my distance from the entire ruckus. We all had left before the police arrived. I was not even fighting, but I got a nice shiner.

I told my friends, "In the future, when we go for drinks, let's go to a local bar in a quiet neighborhood."

I had to sneak home, so my mother would not see my black eye, especially after what she had told me. I was avoiding Mom as much as possible, but my sister Mary told on me. All I could hear Mom saying was, "What is this?" while she was doing the sign of the cross. No matter what I said, she asked what kind of people I hung around with. I tried to explain they had nothing to do with it; it was just a stupid accident. I must have heard about my shiner for weeks.

When Tessie was about to turn sixteen, Mom planned a surprised birthday party. She told me to ask a few of my friends from work. After what happened, I was surprised she would even suggest it.

I knew I could not just invite a few, so instead, I invited most of the guys, and all of them showed up. Mom had a fit because it was a small apartment, so we moved the party to the roof just to accommodate everybody. Thank God it was summer and the weather was just perfect. Plus, it was also a good thing we lived on the top floor. All the guests seemed to be enjoying themselves.

I thought I knew all my sister's friends, but I came across this sexy girl. Before I even got to know her name, my mother told me, "I see you've met your cousin from Greece." This was just my luck.

Now that Tessie had turned sixteen, she was able to go to some of the Greek dances that I attended. Mom made it exceptionally clear she could only go if one of us took her. My brothers never got involved with going to any of these affairs.

Mom was always concerned when I went out. Now that Tessie was also going, it made it that much worse. Now she would tell us both, "*Ta matia sou dekatesita*" (Have fourteen eyes).

Tessie's only drawback was she knew she could not go alone; I had to chaperone her. We got along pretty decently so that made it a lot easier for both of us. What made it even more difficult for me was that Tessie was pretty and sexy. There were times I had to step in when I saw some guys getting a little too personal. She would eventually tell me to lay off when she felt I was overdoing it. I guess the brother in me was too overbearing.

Manhattan Center was on Eighth Avenue and Thirty-Fourth Street. It had been built in 1906 as an opera house. Over the years, it had changed hands. Now this was where they would have most of the Greek dances.

I became friendly with one of the Greek singers. It all started with a drink. I was at the bar when this guy walked up to me; he tapped me on the shoulder and started talking to me in Greek. He said, "Buy me a drink." He thought I was someone else and apologized when he realized his error.

I said to the bartender, "Give him a drink." He thanked me, and we both introduced ourselves. After we had chatted a while, I realized he was one of the famous Greek singers.

From that night, we became friends, and I also found out he loved his spirits (a drink) just before he did his performance.

Jack gave me a whiskey flask for my birthday when I turned eighteen; that was the legal drinking age then. Mom would remark, "Do we have a bum in the family now?" I assured her that would never happen.

I was not a serious drinker and would nurse my drinks. Mom always had some variety of liquor in the china cabinet for when we had company. So I always had an adequate supply when I needed it. My new friend found out about it, and we would have a drink together before he did his performance.

Many times, if I knew would be drinking, I would not drive. Some days, it did not even pay because of parking. When I was alone, I would walk home. This one time, when I was with my sister, we were going home on the bus.

Two pretty girls purposely sat next to us and gave me the look over. I started talking to them, and then I realized they were not interested in me but my sister.

We were getting off at the next stop, so that chapter came to an end, and we never got to know what would have happened. I told Tessie, "This is just a sample of the world we live in."

Mom always stayed up when we went out. Then she would give us the third degree and would want to know if anything exciting happened. Like we would ever tell her everything!

Come vacation time, my friend Raphael from work and I decided to take a trip together. Mom, as usual, said, "Be sure to call when you arrive there."

We got a complete package deal we both could not resist. My friend was easy to please as long as they served beer.

We were going to Ontario, Canada, on a new, experimental jet plane called the Electra (half jet, half prop). It was an experience we will never forget—or at least I will not. We flew out of LaGuardia airport late Friday night.

I was napping by the window when all of a sudden, I was awakened by these flames coming out of one of the engines. In a matter of seconds, some of the passengers were screaming. I was concerned, but I kept my composure. I could not help thinking, *Is this how it ends?*

My friend had been sleeping but woke up with all the shouting and screaming. He shouted, "What is going on?"

I told him one of the engines was on fire. He said, "That's nice," shut his eyes, and dozed off like nothing had happened.

A few seconds later, the pilot announced, "We have to make an emergency landing." The fire was extinguished somehow, and the engine was just smoldering as we were landing.

When we landed, my friend woke up and asked, "We're here already?"

I said, "No, we had to make an emergency landing." I reminded him about the fire.

He said, "What fire? What? I missed all the excitement!" As we disembarked from the plane, many of the passengers were still frantic.

We spent almost three hours there before we boarded another flight, which was an old Constellation prop plane. We arrived in Ontario well past midnight. When we finally checked into the hotel, it was late, so I decided not to call until morning.

Big mistake. When I called, all I got was my mother shouting at me. I should have called no matter what time. I apologized, but she still continued. I just let her get her anger out of her system. To keep Mom happy, I called her every night, hoping to make some peace between us.

The following morning, we started out bright and early. We took a ride into Quebec City to take in the sights. After a day of sightseeing, we had something to eat. We hit just about every nightspot on the main drag.

One day, it was rainy, so we decided to see a movie. The film was *Julia Cesar*. When we sat down, we realized the movie was in French, but as long as my friend had his beer, he was satisfied. There was not much we could do but watch it.

On the last day, we took a boat ride through the St. Lawrence Seaway. We saw sights that were only once in a lifetime. It was a truly memorable experience.

The flight home was a more enjoyable one, at least for me. I came to find out the emergency landing had made the news. I never told my mother anything because I knew how she would react. Years later, that same jet engine plane was no longer in service because of other tragic mishaps.

The funny thing was the car manufacturer Buick named a car the Electra. I hope it runs better than the airplane did.

My brother Jack was one guy who just did his own thing. He would let nothing bother him. As much as Mom hated when he smoked, he told us he was going out to get a pack of cigarettes and got lost.

Then when he finally came home, he did not come alone. He returned with a wife. Mom took it pretty badly; she was in complete withdrawal. Mom never accepted his new wife. She told him that this marriage would never last. I wondered if Mom had put a hex on it, because he got divorced shortly thereafter. One would think after doing it once, he would have learned his lesson.

Not Jack. Years later, he did it again. He eloped. We all felt sorry for Mom; she had to experience it not just once but twice. His new wife's name was Helen; she was a Jewish girl from Brooklyn.

At first, Mom did not accept her, but as time went on, she started to change her attitude. Before we knew it, Mom had started to get along with her, just like she was her own daughter. As for myself, I looked at Helen as an older sister and got to love her just as if she was part of the family.

Working all week, I looked forward to the weekend. If I did not have a date, I went out and hit the town. On some Saturday nights, I would enjoy going out alone. I loved hitting the Greek nightclubs on Ninth Avenue where they had belly dancers.

One Saturday night, I was sitting at the bar nursing a drink. The belly dancer had just started performing when I see this older man get up and start dancing next to her. I had to take a second look. It was one of my uncles. Not wanting to embarrass him, I left and went to another club just across the street.

He had done me a tremendous favor, because I met this beautiful girl. We were hitting it off and having a fabulous time. Suddenly, this man tapped me on my shoulder and asked what I was doing there. I couldn't believe it; it was my uncle. Here I was trying to avoid him, and he spotted me.

We chatted, and I could sense he had had one too many. He made a remark about the girl and asked, "Does your mother know about her?"

I immediately changed the subject and asked, "What are you doing here?"

He told me that every so often he liked to come to the clubs to unwind.

We managed to sneak out and went to another club. I just kept my fingers crossed that I would not run into him again. I told my mother I had seen uncle T at the Greek nightclubs.

The first thing she said was "Was he alone?" Then she laughed it off and made a joke about it. I later came to find out he had told my mother about the girl. As usual, Mom questioned me; I just told her enough to keep her happy.

By sheer accident, I had met a girl whom my sister knew. She was a few years younger than I was. Mom loved her, because she was Greek. From the first day Mom met her, she treated her just like a daughter.

One Saturday, I was taking my car to be washed. I noticed I had a flat tire. Just my luck. And to make matters worse, the spare was also flat.

I took the spare to a gas station to have it fixed. After I had the tire repaired, I started to jack the car up, but the jack was not holding.

I had a date with my new girlfriend, and it was getting late. I had to visit the gas station again to have them take care of the tire. They told me it would be at least an hour.

I called my mother to tell her what had happened. Then I called my girlfriend to tell her the same, and that I would be running late. She gave me a hard time, as if I had wanted all this aggravation.

I should have realized from that moment the kind of girl she was when she gave me that selfish attitude.

Mom was always concerned when we were out, especially since I was a fairly new driver. This I will always remember: One night, well after 1:00 a.m., I was heading home after a date. I was on FDR Drive. It was a little foggy, and traffic was light. There were two cars in front of me, and no one behind me. The first car was in the same middle lane as me, and about twenty car lengths ahead. The second car was about ten lengths ahead in the right lane. Through the fog, and at a distance, I saw headlights coming toward us, which did not look normal.

All of a sudden, this car hit the first car head-on, sending it into the air. It landed on top of the other car, crushing the roof and unfortunately killing the driver. I immediately stopped when I saw the two cars collide. I could not believe what had just happened.

Once I got some of my composure back, I walked up to the car that had been going the wrong direction. The driver was getting out of his car. He walked toward me; his speech was slurred, and he smelled of alcohol. The other driver got pinned in his car and was unable to communicate.

The police, fire engines, and medics came and went straight to help the driver who was pinned in his car. I was still shaking from witnessing this horrible accident. It took almost two hours before traffic was moving again, which was a good thing, because it took that long for me to settle down.

The driver who caused the accident was handcuffed and arrested. I gave the police officer all the details as I had seen them.

When I got home, well after 3:00 a.m., Mom had a fit. She shouted, "You should be ashamed of yourself, coming home at this time." She went on and said, "Your older brothers never came home at this time."

I tried to explain what had happened, that I could not get to a phone.

She went on, and all she said was I should have called. "Don't you ever learn?"

Tessie was awake when this was all happening. She stuck up for me—for the good it did. Mom said if I did it again, she would lock me out. I tried to explain again, but she would not listen.

Another time, we had gone skiing upstate. We started heading home when all of a sudden we ran into a fog. It got so miserable I could just barely see my own hood, much less the road. We saw and witnessed so many accidents, so I stopped at a gas station.

My friend Louis, with whom I had grown up, was living in this area, so I called him. He knew exactly where we were. I told him about the foggy conditions. He replied that he would come and guide us back to his house.

I called home, so they would not worry, but the line was busy. So I decided to call from my friend's house and also told my girlfriend to remind me.

He finally found us. He said he had never seen a fog that dense before. We followed him at a slow speed. As close as we were, I could just barely see his car.

When we got to his house, I tried calling home, but the phone was still busy. The Pappas curse took over. I was so tired I dozed off and did not wake up until the next morning.

The first thing I did when I woke up was call home. The phone rang once, and Tessie answered it. Before I could even talk, Tessie said, "Is that you, Mike?" I explained what had happened and asked her to tell Mom I was okay. It was still foggy, and when it cleared up, I would be on my way.

She told me Mom had just left for church. I was upset with my girlfriend. She called her family and never made an effort to remind me, even after I asked her. Was I asking too much?

We left just shortly after 10:00 a.m. It was still a little foggy in some spots. After I dropped her off, I went home, took a shower, and went to work at church.

Yes, I got a real bawling out. I told Mom the whole story. She was not as angry as I had thought she might be. I gave her a warm hug, and I apologized.

My friends and relatives had read my name in the newspaper. There was a guy about my age with the same name, who was arrested for armed robbery. The phone would not stop ringing, with people thinking it was me. So for a short time, I was a "bad dude."

My friend Gregg had worked for a company that had their own health club. He was able to let family members take advantage.

One summer evening, after we came from the gym, I saw this couple walking toward us at distance holding hands. I said to Gregg, "That girl looks like my girlfriend Pat." Sure enough, I was right. It was she. As soon as she realized I was there, their hands became disengaged.

She immediately asked what I was doing in this neighborhood.

I replied, "We just came from the gym. What are you doing?"

She said, "We are walking home."

I said, "That is a long walk."

She immediately changed the subject, and then she introduced me to her friend. I could sense she felt decidedly uncomfortable talking. Then she had the nerve to say to me, "Do you want to take me home?"

I said, "No, I do not want to interfere with your plans."

What got me upset was she never enjoyed walking more than she had to. Again, you would think I would learn.

There were some days I could swear I had more money than I found in my wallet. I got suspicious of my sister Mary, only because she had asked me for a dollar one day. I had four singles, and I gave her one. I noticed she had a twenty-dollar bill in her wallet. I asked why she wanted it when she had twenty. She replied, deadly seriously, "I do not want to break it, because I'll spend it faster."

I took back my dollar and said, "Break it and spend it."

So I decided to set her up. I carefully took a bunch of loose change and positioned it in my wallet on the inside top. This one morning, bright and early, I was awakened by the loud sound of change falling on the hard floor. Sure enough, there she was standing with my wallet in her hand. She said, "Good morning," as if nothing had happened, and then she was speechless.

I told her, "If you need something, just ask. All I could say is 'No.'"

I started working the day shift, so I was able to take some evening courses at City College. On my school nights, Mom would have super ready; just like when I was working.

One day, as I was getting out of the car, I finished eating some peanuts. I tossed the empty bag into the trash can. I had my supper and was getting ready to hit the sack, so before going to bed. I emptied my pockets like I normally did and put all my change and my wallet on the top of my dresser. I noticed I had put an empty peanut bag on the dresser.

I was thinking to myself, *I thought I threw the wrapper in the trash can. Where is the twenty-dollar bill I had in my pocket earlier?* I realized just then that, like an idiot, I must have thrown the twenty-dollar bill in the trash instead of the peanut bag. I immediately ran downstairs half-dressed hoping to find it where I had carelessly thrown it.

I was happy; it was just lying rolled up on top of the other trash. It is one thing to spend it foolishly, but what I had done was not too smart.

Another time, as I was walking up the stairs after coming from school, I saw two firemen coming down the stairs, one carrying a fire extinguisher. It was our apartment they were coming out of. It seems while Mom was warming up my supper, the oven caught fire because of grease that had accumulated over the years. Thank God everybody was okay, and there was no serious damage.

In 1960, I voted for the first time. Being we grew up in a Democratic Party environment, I was exceptionally influenced.

John Kennedy inspired me by the way he spoke. I will always remember one famous comment he made: "Ask not what your country can do for you; ask what you can do for your country." That comment stuck with me. I also felt because he was a war hero, he could do a lot for the country.

As I was growing up, I realized it was not the party that made the person, but the person himself. Was I too young and inexperienced to feel the way I did? It was also incredible how over the years, I learned about the world of politics, how politicians all made promises and that was where it ended. When they got in office, all their promises all of a sudden were forgotten or put on the back burner. Some things in life never change, but stay the same.

Mary loved going to Greece for her vacation. She always purchased gold while she was there, because the dollar would buy a lot more. We always told her she had a big mouth, because she was always bragging about her gold jewelry.

Well, I guess someone else wanted some of her gold. When we were all out, someone broke into the apartment, which was easier than going to Greece. She had an idea who it was, but that was as far as that went. One would think she would have learned her lesson, but not Mary, she would continue to say too much. I guess some people never learn.

In the earlier sixties, a new trend started. The people who followed it were called hippies or beatniks. Years later, the trend spread worldwide; it was hard to explain the life they led. They lived a totally different lifestyle, from health food to the music festival to contemporary sexual mores. They even had their own way of speaking and expressing themselves.

I remember Mom always making comments about the way they lived and their lifestyle. I told her that was what made this country so admired and superb: anybody could express his or her own way of living.

Mom was always curious and could sense things; I guess it was in her. One day, maybe it was by accident, but Tessie's handbag fell on the floor and out fell a wedding band. Mom immediately picked it up and said, "What is this?" She shouted angrily, "Did you do a stupid thing and get married?" Mom was all over her. I felt sorry for Tessie, and I came to her rescue.

Mom was a bundle of nerves—first Jack, now Tessie. She was in a state of total shock. I tried to calm her down, but she just went on and on, while doing the sign of the cross. She called the pastor, Father Kazanas, to try to get some comfort.

Years earlier, Tessie had been dating a Greek fellow named Peter, who passed away. She had been through a lot, so I tried to give her support. My brothers and sister Mary were not as supportive.

The fellow she had married was an Italian immigrant named Sam, who had come into the country illegally. He had jumped ship; so in order to stay, he had to get married to an American citizen.

The law then was he had to return to his native country and then return legally. I looked back and thought about what our parents and all the other immigrants who came to this country had to endure. Not to mention new arrivals had to go for a blood test to be sure that they were free of sickness or disease and spend at least one full day at Ellis Island before they could stay here legally. Oh boy, how times have changed!

When I first met Sam, I had mixed emotions, but over the years, he became just like one of the family. Eventually, Mom even came around and started to display affection for him like he was a son and made him feel like part of the family.

With Jack and Harry both married and now Tessie moving out of the house, it was not the same. I think Mom missed not having us all together. I know I did.

Even though, Mom always complained about being tried. Come Sundays and holidays, she just loved to do her thing and cook up a feast. Mom was always the nucleus, because she kept us all together and close as a family.

Tessie and Sam found their own apartment. They wanted to express their gratitude, so they invited all of us for a Sunday dinner.

Sam loved to cook and made a delightful Italian-American home-style meal. They also spent a lot of time getting their apartment fixed up, especially to show Mom. Sam was like Jack and loved to buy expensive clothing.

At dinner, Sam told us about an incident that had just happened. He was getting home from work, and as he was walking up the stairs, he saw this fellow carrying a box with a suit that resembled his. In fact, they both said hello to each other.

When he got home, he noticed the door was open a crack. He ran inside and noticed that someone had been in there. Sure enough, he realized that suit that guy was holding was his. Without wasting another second, Sam ran after him, but with no luck; he had just disappeared. All I could say was welcome to America.

In 1961, Mom became a grandmother, and I became an uncle. Harry and Lillian had their first daughter, whom they named Karen. It was a tremendous thing for Mom because it gave her a spiritual lift in life.

Jack and Helen could not have children of their own. They had adopted a boy whom they named Jon. As the years passed, many other grandchildren came into her life.

Jack had been a key member of the Playboy Club ever since they opened on Fifty-Ninth Street. He was very meticulous about lending the key out. I asked to borrow the key, and he hesitated at first, but he eventually let me use it. Somehow, Mom caught on, and she would blast me for going to a place of that character.

Chapter 11

Getting Away

My friend Gregg and I got invited to a lot of parties. The friends that I had made from the conversation invited us to a party. We went to many parties locally, but the best was when we got invited to one out of town. Now the downside was that it was in Detroit, Michigan. It sounded crazy to drive so far for just a party. We were always doing crazy things, so this fit right into our social calendar. We even asked our friend Bill; he thought we were crazy and declined.

I laugh every time I think back, and I say one has to be young and daring, maybe even crazy, to do the things we did. I told my mother and my girlfriend I was going away for the weekend with my friend Gregg.

I never told them it was just to go to a party. I know my girlfriend would have been against it. My mother would have called us both crazy, and she would have been right.

We were going to leave after work on Friday and hoped to be in Detroit Saturday morning. We planned everything; we rotated drivers in two-hour shifts, hoping to keep from getting tired.

I will never forget, we were on the Queen Elizabeth Highway in Canada heading into Detroit. I was taking a nap; somehow, I woke up and noticed the car was swerving. I was rubbing my eyes, and I looked over to say something. I was in total shock; he had fallen asleep at the wheel.

It was as if God was watching over us. I grabbed the steering wheel, carefully pulled over to the side of the highway, and brought the car to a complete and safe stop, and then I woke my sleeping friend.

Thank God there were no other cars around us. He woke up in a daze, never realizing where he was. I told him to get some shut-eye, and I took over and let him rest a while. After driving all night and into the morning, we finally made it to Detroit.

We were both like zombies. We found a motel and decided to take a short nap. Later, we decided to check the area out. One thing led to another, and before we realized it, we were out most of the day. We took another nap to rest up for the party. We were both so exhausted that we overslept. We never woke up until Sunday morning.

We ate breakfast with a few of them and told them what had happened. We thanked them for inviting us just the same. A few hours later, we started back home well rested. We got home a little after midnight. For a party we never made it to, we both agreed that was a party we would never forget.

My friend Gregg and I had done a lot of traveling over the years to different places, including Canada, parts of the South, like New Orleans, and the Midwest as far as Texas. We had some exciting moments. When we were in Oklahoma on one of the trips, we came across a twister in the distance. Let me say it was a tense feeling not knowing which way it would be moving. Just as fast as it appeared, it disappeared, but the most memorable time was when we drove to Mexico.

Both our parents never liked it when we took these travel vacations. When we told them about Mexico, they were even more upset. Up to the last minute, they always tried to talk us out of going. I explained that I worked all year so that I would be able to enjoy a pleasant vacation. Once I settled down, this would all be but a memory.

Gregg had just bought a brand-new 1962 Pontiac Bonneville. It was a white convertible with a red interior. We both had two weeks' vacation, so we decided to drive down in style. Being on a strict budget, we stayed at the cheapest motel we could find.

We left home at the crack of dawn and drove all day and into the night. It was getting late, so we decided to call it a day. We came into this small town called Gadsden in Alabama. It was dark and later than we wanted.

The motel we stayed in was in a secluded location. After we checked in, I said, "Does this motel remind you of somewhere? Guess who is not taking a shower."

Both our mothers never enjoyed it when we traveled. They had just one request: that we would call them often. We would use that famous strategy of calling collect and asking for yourself to save money.

We could not find a pay phone that worked. To top it off, we could not even find a place to grab a bite to eat. So all we could do was eat some junk food.

The whole area was like a desert. There was nothing to do but watch TV, and after a while, we finally called it a night.

After we turned in, we heard strange noises, and there was this red light coming through the blinds. It was difficult to try to get some peaceful shut-eye. We figured out that it was the motel's neon sign that was making the red reflection. The noises continued; we were trying to figure out what was making the noise.

Had I seen too many movies? We secured a chair behind the door, just to be on the safe side. We were not taking any chances. I looked through the blinds and noticed something strange. There were no other cars in the parking section except ours. We finally fell asleep, but not for long, At about 4:00 a.m., we heard more strange noises.

I said, "Let's get out of here; we grabbed the luggage and took off. We never looked back. We drove until the sun came up, and then we had breakfast. We called home, so our families would not worry.

After that, we made sure we stopped early just to be sure we found a safe and suitable motel. No more budget motels for us. You get what you pay for!

We stopped at my friend Gayle's home; she had her own pad just outside of Dallas. She would have one of her friends couple up with Gregg. We spent the evening together. The following morning, we had a late breakfast and were on our way; it was only about six hours to Brownsville, Texas. The best part was we were just a few miles from the Mexican border.

We had dinner and spoke to many people who told us the same story. Be extremely careful while driving in Mexico. "Do not drive when it gets dark." There were bandits, and as soon as it got dark, they would block the roads with their cars or trucks and rob tourists. It was about a twelve-hour trip to get to Mexico City, so we had to stop somewhere halfway.

We got stopped several times by the Mexican police to check the car and IDs. It was as if they were calling ahead purposely, just to throw their weight around. They had pearl-handled forty-fives, and believe me, we were not going make them mad. Was this racial profiling?

The main road was the Pan American Highway. By the way, it sounded like it was a double-lane, blacktopped road. The surprise was it was a single lane with nothing but gravel and dirt.

There were times we could not drive more than forty miles. To top it off, we were lucky if we saw another car. We had to drive over the mountains in order to get to Mexico City. After driving a while, we could see them on the horizon.

Gas stations were limited on this road, and for a while, we were concerned. We had driven until about six o'clock. We were not taking any chances, after hearing about the alleged Mexican bandits.

We found a quaint Mexican villa to spend the night at. To save time in the morning, we gassed up. The car started making this strange pinging sound.

We had dinner, and we met some other Americans, who told us not to drink the water. They warned us to be sure it was only out of a bottle and make sure it was imported and the bottle was sealed.

The next morning, we started out extra early, skipping breakfast to save time. We started heading up the mountain with the car pinging even louder. Gregg was driving; we were snacking on some junk food. As we were driving, we got stuck behind an extremely slowly moving school bus. If we were doing fifteen miles per hour, we were lucky.

The road was too narrow to try to pass, so all we could do was continue following the bus up the mountain and around sharp curves; it looked as if we were driving into the sky.

We were near the top, and the school bus driver gave us a motion to pass him. We went around the school bus and around the curve. There was a large gasoline trailer truck coming right at us.

Again, God was watching over us, and we swerved out of the way just in time. The car came to a dead stop. There were no guardrails or anything. I could look straight down about four thousand feet. The tires were resting directly on the edge, and we could hear the dirt moving from under the tires. I told Gregg to move slowly away from the edge.

Gregg started moving away, and we could literally hear the dirt and stones falling from under the tires. When we finally made it to the top of the mountain, we found a location to relax a spell. I think our hearts were in our mouths after that close encounter.

As we were enjoying the view, out of nowhere, natives started to gather all around us. Not knowing what to expect, I told Gregg, "Let's get the heck out of here."

We jumped into the car, and then drove off in a cloud of dust. We finally made it down the mountain, the car still pinging. We came across some road construction; the police were rerouting the traffic onto a side path, which we drove slowly on for a few miles. It must have rained earlier because the grassy road was wet and muddy.

We got back on the main road, which was blacktop, only to discover the car was racing. We were both saying, "What happened now?" It seems when we were driving on the grassy side road, the bottom of the car was too low, causing it to break the shifting gear into low gear.

Now we had a new car making pinging sounds and the engine racing and getting hot, and here we were a thousand miles from home.

We were lucky my cousin through marriage Steve was in Mexico City on business. He had said to call him when we arrived and we would have dinner.

So we called him when we got to the hotel. We explained what had happened, and he said he would make a phone call and get back to us.

At this point, we wondered if it was the end of the vacation. He called us back and told us he had gotten ahold of a mechanic who would be coming shortly. He told us to stay with the car.

So we waited patiently for someone to meet us; this monumental old black Cadillac limousine pulled up in front of the car. Three guys came out; one looked like a big businessman; the others wore work clothes and were covered with grease. The man with the suit walked up to us. We spoke to him and told him what had happened. He told his two other men to check the car.

We had no notion what to expect. After a few minutes, they started talking among themselves in their native tongue.

After they finished talking, the boss walked up to us and said we had enormous problems, but not to worry. He told us it would cost two hundred to fix it. We looked at each other; our mouths fell to the floor when we heard the price.

He said, "Relax. That is only twenty dollars in American money." You never saw two happier guys when we heard that. They took out some tools and a blowtorch from their trunk and fixed the car right where it was. Before we knew it, they had finished, and he said, "It is as close as new," but if we wanted to feel more confident to have it checked out when we got back home.

We told him about the pinging sound coming out of the engine. He told us also the gas in Mexico was not the same octane as it is in the States. Since our car was a high performance one, that made matters even worse.

The car was no longer racing or getting hot, but the pinging was still there. He said to try to avoid high speeds until we got back into the States. Once we got new gas in the car, the pinging sound should disappear. We finally checked in at the hotel to rest.

We ate dinner that night with my cousin and thanked him. Later, he took us out on the town. We spent a few days in Mexico City. We took in some sights and saw a few bullfights. The locals would watch bullfighting like we watched ball games. The stadium held over forty thousand and was filled to capacity. Then we learned it was nothing but a public slaughterhouse, so unless one enjoyed seeing blood, it was not recommended.

The next stop was Acapulco. It was only a four-hour ride, so we ate a late breakfast and were on our way. The ocean view was breathtaking as we were heading into Acapulco. The region was beautiful until we saw the city itself; it was a ghetto if we had ever seen one. We were told to stay out of the city if we liked being healthy. We might be from a large city, but we didn't need a brick to fall on us.

So we stayed away and made the best of it at the hotel. We spent a few days around the hotel complex and went to the beach, where we would feel a little safer. Between the bars, the pool, the beach, and the girls, we kept ourselves busy.

We met some girls at the pool who had just flown in that morning from New York. I was attracted to one of them. After talking with her, I came to discover she lived just one block from where I lived. To top it off, her house number was exactly the same. How bizarre is that? She had been living there almost her whole life. What a small world, that we could run into each other here.

She had attended Catholic school while she was growing up; that was one reason why we had never crossed paths in school. I also came to discover she was engaged, and that sure busted my bubble.

Since we both would stroke out, we agreed that we should start thinking about heading home; for a while, we thought about sending the car back and flying home. The problem was the cost was astronomical, so that ended that idea.

So we left a day earlier than planned, mainly because we were still concerned with the long journey home. The mechanic was not entirely wrong; it was still pinging but not as often. We drove more and made fewer stops, keeping the speed down. Our advice to anybody who ever wants to drive into Mexico is don't.

Chapter 12

My Life Changes

Shortly after we returned from vacation, Gregg and I both got our draft notices. I knew it was going to happen someday, but when you get that greeting from Uncle Sam, it changes your whole world besides sending a chill.

Before I left for the service, my family and friends threw me a going-away party. To top it off, I also got in engaged. Mom was not thrilled about me being drafted. As much as she tried to fight it, she knew it was out of our hands. On the positive side, she was extremely pleased that I had gotten engaged to a Greek girl named Patricia.

I did my basic training and advanced training at Fort Dix, New Jersey. I noticed they had my first name wrong. They had Michael instead of Mike, which was my true and legal name. I remember at the briefing the sergeant saying, "Make sure everything is correct and in order because Uncle Sam does not make mistakes."

Ha, ha. My mother got wind of this and got worried. She said, "Do not make trouble with the government."

So I immediately told the first sergeant about the mistake; he said I was out of order. He loudly said, "Your legal name is Michael and not Mike."

I said, "Not to be disrespectful, but you are wrong. Please have my name corrected."

He called me a few choice words and said, "Dismissed."

I went back at him and said, "Okay, I'll go to other channels to have it corrected."

I went to see the commanding officer of my unit. I told him the whole story. He asked why I had waited so long to have this corrected.

"I told the first sergeant about it the first day, and he ignored it. And it took till now to get to see you, sir."

He said, "I need your original birth certificate. Once I have it, I can make the correction."

I called home to tell them the story. I told them to give my birth certificate to Pat, so that when she came on Sunday she could give it to me. My mother again said, "Do not make any problems with the government." There she went worrying about that. I told her not to worry, that what I was doing was correct.

Monday morning, I brought it to my commanding officer. He told me he would take care of it. Well, I guess my first sergeant found out what I had done, and let me say, it was hell for the next few weeks.

He never told me verbally about it, but he started picking on me for everything and never let up. He was on me like a bee on honey; for example, he made me shave even though I had no facial hairs. To top it off, he made me shave using cold water only. Then he claimed my rifle was dirty even though I had just cleaned it. He went on to put me on KP, even though I had already pulled it twice in the same week.

The worst was the first weekend's leave, he put me on a particular assignment. I had had it. I had done nothing to deserve this harassment. Unfortunately, since I was in the service, there was not much I could do but take it.

The commanding officer paid the unit a surprise inspection. We were all at attention in front of the bunk beds, and as he was walking past me with the first sergeant on his heels, he stopped right in front of me and said out loud, "Pappas, you realize it cost Uncle Sam hundreds of dollars, maybe even a thousand, to correct your first name?"

I replied, "If someone were doing his job, it might have been avoided, sir."

He told the sergeant, "You better take even more care of Pappas. Uncle Sam has extra money invested in him." After that remark, he made a total about-face with me. Maybe I was being too cautious, but I was not taking any chances.

I made many new friends from the tri-state area. A few of us became close, almost like brothers. Even they could see the extra pressure the first sergeant had put on me. For the first few weekends of basic training, we only got Sundays off. It did not pay to go home with only one day off, so Pat came down on Sundays to see me for a few hours.

This was the only time I got to see her until I got a full weekend off. Pat met a lot of my new army buddies and their families. Thereafter, I made sure I went home every weekend.

Harry had been in the army, and he told me never to volunteer my time, no matter what they promised. He was so correct, because I never did, and I had more time to myself. Many guys who had gracefully volunteered found themselves getting screwed and missing out on passes.

During basic training, Uncle Sam gave us a series of tests to determine everybody's job occupation. After we got the final results, my assessment was communications.

A few guys were lucky and were staying Stateside. Most of us were being shipped out of the States. I got my orders, and they had a California PO box number. My exact job and destination were still a surprise. My friend Gregg went to Germany.

I was going to the Far East, and that was all I knew. I was off for the weekend, and I had to be in California to catch a flight out on Monday morning from Travis Air Force Base. I spent Friday and Saturday with Pat and left Sunday morning. I was somewhat nervous, still not knowing my exact destination. I was extremely fortunate that I was going by air. I later found out some guys who volunteered for the service went by ship. The government works in strange ways.

We flew on this vast military transport; we were sitting backward on these hard seats. It felt like being on the New York City subway. The only enjoyable part of the flight was we had a layover in Hawaii. It was the strangest phenomenon; we left on Monday morning and did not arrive in Japan until Wednesday. With all the time traveling, we lost Tuesday, because of the international date line.

When we landed in Japan, I had to switch over to another plane, still not knowing my exact destination; at this point, it did not matter.

We landed at a military air base just outside of Seoul, Korea. Once we departed, we went to an airplane hangar where we eventually loaded on to different trucks. The unfortunate part was nobody knew what their destination was. I thought I was in hell; for the first time in my adult life, I was scared. My first thought was I would never see home again. Then to make matters worse, there was this awful smell. It was something I had never thought existed.

While we were getting instructions, we had to exchange any US currency for what they called MPC (military payment certificates). I came to realize the US government did not want the American dollar to get into the hands of the Korean people. The government was so strict that if you were caught with US currency in your possession, you could be criminally charged. Without warning, they would put every unit in a lockup and change the MCP, leaving the old ones worthless. Anyone who possessed the old MCP was totally out of luck; it was as useless as play money.

A few of the guys would do their duty up toward the border of North Korea. I lucked out; I got assigned to a headquarters battalion. The unit was about ten miles south of the demilitarized zone (DMZ) border of North Korea, which is a 2.5-mile buffer zone separating the two Koreas.

When we got to the unit, we were all assigned brackets. Shortly thereafter, we got our orientation and our job assignments. I got assigned to communication but had no clue what to expect.

Since I was fresh from the States, I got the worst job possible. I went on line duty. That meant every time a telephone line went out, which was virtually every day, I had to go out and repair it. The only enjoyable part of the job was we were exempt from KP and guard duty.

One of the friends I met in basic training, Vinnie, was going to work as a chef for the officers' club. He would many times make dinner for both of us after the officers had their dinner. The best part was we ate using real china and not metal trays. Sometimes we even had steak, which was unheard of. Maybe Korea was not going to be as miserable as I had first thought.

Since I was going to spend thirteen months there, I decided I would educate myself on the country's culture. The Japanese had occupied Korea from 1910 until 1945. Then, in 1945, the Soviets forced the Japanese up the peninsula to what is the thirty-eighth parallel, which divided the country in half. There were many border skirmishes, but in June of 1950, the north invaded the south, which brought on the beginning of the Korean Conflict.

The war raged on for three years, and then on July 27, 1953, an armistice was signed. The sad part was over a quarter of a million civilians lost their lives, but there is no actual count because many died from illness. More than thirty-six thousand American troops died in action, not including the thousands missing in action and those who died in other mishaps; over ninety-two thousand were wounded. Now, just ten years later, I was there to serve my part.

The weather there was like back home; the only real difference was the rain. When it rained there, it was always a monsoon. The funny thing was, shortly after the rain, everything was dry as a bone. One would think it had not rained for months. Most of the natives who lived outside of the large cities lived in wooden huts. Electricity was limited in many parts of the country. I had never seen so much poverty in my life before, and I thought I had seen it all.

On Sundays, when I was off, I would take the bus to the city of Seoul. I came across a Korean Orthodox Church; the services were just like back home except for two things: the service was in Korean, and there were no seats.

Donating Icons

I got to meet some soldiers and a family. I also met a CIA agent, who was on special assignment. We would all chat, as if we were old friends. The father was the assistant to the American ambassador, and he invited us to his home for a Sunday brunch. All of a sudden, Sundays felt like being home.

Our unit was assisting one of the local orphanages. It was incredible the things you learned firsthand when you were at the source. I came to discover for every dollar that was donated, ten cents went to the children, with so-called administration expenses and etc. What's wrong with that picture?

There were so many children who where abandoned for different reasons, which upset me. It did not take me long before I became attached to this young boy named Park. His story was a sad one. He had been abandoned by a trash can, because of his skin color. He was left to die, but by the grace of God, some soldiers took him to the orphanage.

I started taking him when I was off duty. I was teaching him some English, and in return, I was learning some Korean. I would take him to the recreation room at the unit where we could watch TV. Park became mesmerized watching it and got to love baseball. He became interested, so I bought him a glove and a bat and ball.

At one point, I had wanted to adopt him. The problem was with all the crazy and complemented paperwork, it never panned out. I always wondered if I had done it, how my mother or Pat would have reacted.

There was a running brook at the rear of the camp. Many of us would go for a swim or just to chill off. Then we discovered not too far up the stream, the locals would bathe, wash clothing, and even dump their waste. That ended our desire for any more dips.

After all these years, I finally learned to drive a shift stick. Every few weeks, we would rotate the midnight shift. Normally, that shift was quiet. It was just my luck when I had that shift for the first time, we had a serious emergency; one of the main phone lines was out.

To make matters even more exciting, this was my first solo call. All I had for light was the headlights from the truck and a spotlight, which I came to find out half of the time did not work. My luck continued. There was no moonlight. It was so dark I could just barely see.

Everything was on top of poles, supposedly to make it more difficult for anyone to steal the wire, but that did not stop the thefts.

It was a must to get it back in working order as soon as possible. It took a while, but I finally found the problem. I got one side connected, and I started climbing the second pole. Just as I was climbing, I could feel something was not right. Being so dark, I could not see the condition of the pole. I was being extra careful, when all of a sudden, my one foot slipped. It seemed the pole was so chewed up it did not hold my climbing spike. I slid all the way down. Thank God for my safety belt. Now we knew why we called it a "safety belt."

Orphanages

Friend and I taking Park and two other children for the day

I had splinters from my knees to my chest and everyplace in between! I was in real pain, but I had to get it fixed no matter what. I finally fixed it and then reported to the infirmary to get all the splinters removed.

With all the pain, I encountered the best part of the whole ordeal: I had a pretty nurse who removed most of the splinters. Must I say any more?

The sergeant and I became close friends, and shortly after my mishap, I asked him to please take me off line duty. He told me I was in luck because one of the guys was heading back to the States in a few weeks because his tour of duty was up.

He gave me my wish, and I went into the radio bunker. What a great feeling it was to change from climbing to sitting. I could get to love this.

I was never a true coffee drinker until then. Getting fresh milk and trying to keep it cold was almost impossible during the warm weather, and getting sugar was not easy. So I got into the habit of drinking it black. Believe me when I say, it kept me awake.

I was trying to call home by using the telephone switchboard from the bunker. All the guys wished me good luck, because even they had had no success. I could only do it when I was working the graveyard shift, because of the time difference. I do not know how I managed, but I got through to Pat. We spoke briefly, and the connection was lost. That was the first and last time, because I could never do it again.

The word came down that anybody who wanted to extend his or her tour of duty had to do it now. A few guys did. As much as I enjoyed my new friends, I just wanted to get home.

One thing I learned about while I was in the service was the importance of timing. Sometimes being in the wrong spot could get one killed; it could also work in one's favor. Within two months after I arrived in Korea, I earned a stripe. Two months later, I earned another, and before I realized it, I had made the grade of E-5. The bunker boss's time was up, and he was returning to the States, so I got his job.

Every few months, someone was heading home, and we would get a replacement. One of the guys who arrived from the States just happened to live in New Jersey and was also bunking in my barracks. He was an exceptionally intelligent fellow; it was common sense and street smarts that he lacked.

The first sergeant was all over him because he made us all look awful as a group. He was never prepared; he never polished things like his shoes or his belt buckle and never even kept his rifle properly cleaned.

So I became the "bad guy" and had to teach him how to prepare for inspection. It was a challenge, but I think I got to him, though he was not totally the way I would want him. As I learned, in life, be thankful, even for the little things.

We finally looked decent for inspection, and it made the sergeant somewhat pleased. Plus, it gave me a pleasant feeling of accomplishment. One point I did learn was one could never make a first sergeant totally satisfied.

We had another fellow assigned to the barracks, who had also just arrived from the States. He was from the Deep South and was as large as a refrigerator.

His first night, there was a horrible body odor smell, and everybody was complaining. It was also the middle of a heat wave, making it that much worse. We came to discover it was the new refrigerator that was causing the odor. Again, I was going to be the "bad guy" who had to tell him about his odor problem.

I politely told him about his personnel hygiene. He then got up and told me, "I do not care what you think." He literally picked me up like a toy. Almost all the guys came to my rescue, and then we all grabbed him and gave him a genuine GI shower. We managed to clean him up, even though he gave us a hard time. After we scrubbed him down, I asked him where his changes of clothing were. He said, "They are coming with my other items by boat." It was hard to believe he had no change of underwear until his hold baggage came, which could take anywhere from two to three weeks.

He had no money, so a few of us chipped in and bought him some. We convinced him that bathing was a must if he did not want any repeat performances.

Break in the action

When I had made bunker boss, I was required to qualify for carrying a firearm. So I went to this shooting range up near the DMZ. After we finished, a few of us took a tour of the area; it was something to see.

Looking into the DMZ, you could see tanks and other armored vehicles from both sides that were destroyed during the conflict. There were many Americans, United Nations, and enemy soldiers who died in this region. It was a strange feeling to witness it; it was as if you could sense their spirits.

I was not on duty but a few hours before all hell broke out. My shift started out pretty quiet, but all of a sudden, we got an emergency alert. I will never forget that time: November 22, 1963, the day that President Kennedy was assassinated.

I was on radio watch; the time was about 2:00 a.m. Saturday morning because of the time difference when it first came over the air that the president had been assassinated. At first, I thought they meant the president of Korea, but then it came over again, saying the president of the United States had been assassinated.

I was in shock; a chill went through me. We went into in a state of emergency. Everybody went on combat-ready status. The hardest part was we had no clue what to expect.

We remained in a state of emergency for almost a week. All I was thinking about was a million North Koreans coming across the thirty-eighth parallel. Finally, things got back to normal—if one can call anything normal there. I was still a little reluctant because we heard radio transmissions about a lot of North Koreans trying to infiltrate across the border. The trouble was the North Koreans would sometimes sneakily broadcast over our frequency to throw us off. This was why we used different codes to avoid false transmissions.

Just before Thanksgiving, my mother sent me an early Christmas care package. It had all the goodies that made me feel at home. It was amazing how many new buddies I made when they got to taste my mother's *"Koulourakia"* (butter cookies). I had to hide some if I was going to enjoy them another day. No matter how much she sent me, it was never enough.

My brother Harry would write me on occasion, but this one time, he sent me a letter with some shocking news. He hated to tell me this, but he felt I should learn about it now. It seems the priest from our church was involved in a scandal. It turned out that he had been with another woman.

When he gave me the details, I was in total shock. He of course had to step down as spiritual leader. That had to be one of the most upsetting letters I could ever receive.

Thanksgiving Message

The necessity for keeping the defenses of our nation strong and alert has placed you a long way from home on a holiday that is traditionally a family affair. Your family, along with millions of other Americans, will thank God this day that you protect our country.

Traditionally, Thanksgiving stands for your neighborhood church, friends and family, the smell of fall in the air, your favorite college football game, turkey and pumpkin pie. But it also stands for much more . . . a nation founded on the principles of a hard won freedom, a nation of plenty with equal opportunities for all. We thank God this Thanksgiving that there have been in the past and that there are those now willing to risk all that they hold dear that it might remain so. Thanksgiving is an American holiday and you are celebrating it in the finest possible way.

Arthur J. Phelan
Capt.   Arty.
Commanding

THANKSGIVING DINNER

Shrimp Cocktail
Cocktail Sauce
Roast Tom Turkey
Cornbread Dressing   Giblet Gravy
Cranberry Sauce
Baked Ham w/Raisin Sauce
Mashed Potatoes
Sweet Potatoes w/Apples
Buttered Peas   Buttered Corn
Assorted Crisp Relishes
Cloverleaf Rolls
Butter
Mince Pie   Pumpkin Pie
Holiday Ice Cream
Candies   Assorted Fresh Fruits   Nuts
Coffee   Tea
Milk

As much as I was enjoying my tour of duty, spending the holidays there was not the same. The headquarters kitchen would make a home-style Thanksgiving spread with all the fixings, hoping to make it feel like home.

After nine months and just before the Christmas holidays, I received a letter from my fiancée. This letter was different; it was a "Dear John." I guess I had spoken too soon.

I was in shock, mostly because had I never seen that coming. I took it pretty hard, but if it had happened when I first got there I might have reacted a little differently.

I had no one close I could turn to; it was a feeling of emptiness. Then to top it off, a new song had just been recorded. I felt like it was meant for me, and every time I heard it, a chill went through me. The song went "This diamond ring does not shine anymore."

I also later found out my family thought that I had met a Korean girl and I had broken it off. How rumors get started! The worst part was being halfway around the world. I could not even defend myself.

Months earlier, one of the new guys who had just arrived from the States received a Dear John letter. While he was on guard duty, he put his rifle to his head and ended it.

I took being engaged extremely seriously. There were many times I had the opportunity to fool around, but I never did. Some of my buddies would tease me by saying this was what I got for being a decent guy.

Maybe I was being too overcautious, but I had seen so many fellows come down with some pretty severe cases of VD (venereal disease). With only a few months, I was not taking any foolish chances.

I started to go to the village that was close to the unit. I was being extremely picky. I wanted my own girlfriend. I had no luck; maybe I was being too picky. But that was just how I was.

Christmas was a very depressing time of year there, especially after my Dear John letter. We all would make the most of it. As they say in Korean, "*Sung Tan Chuk Ha*" (Merry Christmas).

All units had to spend one week strictly in the outdoors as a survival course. So we all packed up and went to a secluded area just below the thirty-eighth parallel. All we had was just a personal tent, a sleeping bag, and K rations to eat. Any food we did not finish, we had to bury.

The saddest episode I ever saw was children and their parents digging up the food we had buried earlier. We were told not to feed them because it would cause problems. Being a softy and remembering years earlier that my older friend told me he could not stand seeing this, I went against the captain's orders. Because of that, I almost got stampeded with the other families when I gave this one family my K rations.

The captain saw this and came down real hard on me. He read me the riot act. (In his words, he "blasted" me.) He repeated himself and said, "Don't you listen?"

I told him I understood why now. I apologized for being so thickheaded. I learned some things that day: one is never too old to learn, and things are said for a reason.

It was the heart of January, and the actual temperature was anywhere from -20 to 0 for a high. Then to make matters worse, we had a snowstorm, which made survival even more of a challenge; with the wind gusts, it was even more brutal. Some of the guys developed frostbite and some got it rather severely.

Even though I came from a relatively cold-winter climate, I had never felt this cold in my life before. There were nights I thought I was not going to survive. One thing I did learn was it is astonishing how quickly you learn to survive the freezing weather. It felt more like a month than a week. I prayed each night for the courage to come out of this.

The first night I had taken off my fatigues and hung them up. The next morning, they were frozen stiff; let me say, putting on a frozen piece of clothing is no joke. Again, it is unbelievable how fast you learn to keep your belongings in your sleeping bag.

When we got back to camp, I thanked God. I never thought I would say this, but it felt fantastic to get back to my drooping bunk bed.

When we got back, I took a trip with one of the guys to another unit southeast of Seoul. It was half work and half relaxation. Once we completed the business part, we took a ride to the coast to tour the region. Big mistake. We ran into a downpour that made the road impassable. We took other roads that led us into dead ends. Then to make matters worse, we ran out of gas and the reserve tank was also empty. One of us had to stay with the jeep or risk it being stolen. We flipped a coin. I didn't know which would be worse: staying or walking. My friend walked back to the base just to get enough gas to get us back on the road. Another lesson in life: whenever you drive to an unknown location, be sure to check that you have a full tank.

I was still somewhat depressed by my Dear John letter. Many times, I would be daydreaming while I was walking back to my unit. Sometimes I would take a shortcut through the rice paddies, just so I could think. One evening while I was heading back to my unit, I got attacked from behind. I managed to fight off the attacker. When I came face-to-face with the so-called attacker, I found it was a large, ugly woman. She said in her broken English, "Hey, GI, want to have a terrific time?"

I yelled out, "No way," and just continued.

Another time while I was walking, I smelled smoke and heard crying. I ran in that direction and saw a hut on fire. There was this young girl with this older man trying to put out the fire. I grabbed a bucket and ran over to this water hole that was partly frozen. I must have run a dozen times dumping this icy water on the hut before we finally got it out.

The girl gave me an enormous hug. She kept repeating in her native tongue, "Thank you."

With my poor Korean, I replied, *"Ju welkam"* (You're welcome).

They were so thankful that even with their home half burned, they wanted me to stay and eat. I tried to make them understand I had to get back to my unit. It took a while, but I finally convinced them I would be back.

I was teaching her English, and her grandfather was teaching me some martial arts. With all the new friends and now this, I was in no hurry to get back to the States. I tried to get an extension to stay longer, but I had missed the deadline.

In the short time I spent with them, he taught me some of their native cultural values. I later came to discover both her parents had been killed during the latter part of the war. Her grandparents had had to raise her, and her grandmother had just recently died.

I would many times take my little friend Park with me. At first, they were not too thrilled because of his biological difference. I tried to make them understand he was just like me, from a different way of living.

He would help me with a few things that they needed to get them back on their feet. They saw how he was helping with some of the work, and their attitude toward him changed.

They always wanted me to try the food that they made. Over the past months, I had been able to see many of their native foods, and the majority of it was aged in the ground. That was that awful smell I had first encountered when I arrived here.

Instead, I would bring some tasty, old-fashioned American food like pizza and hot dogs, which they came to love and enjoy.

Once in a while, we would get a surprise inspection during the midnight shift from this new lieutenant. Sometimes it was so quiet we could take a nap while we were on duty. One of my crew had a habit of doing just that and got caught by the lieutenant.

He tried to have him court-martialed, but the commanding officer talked him out of it. The lieutenant swore if he ever caught one of us doing it again, he would go through with the court-martial.

One of the guys said, "If he does it again, we will be ready for him." It seems the lieutenant had crawled through the emergency exit, which was only four by four instead of coming through the bunker entrance, when he caught the last guy. So he decided to set him up; he put small pieces of barbwire on the floor. So now if he decided to come through the emergency exit again, he was in for a "screaming surprise."

Sure enough, I was on watch this one night; I was resting my eyes. I must have dozed off because I was awakened by some screaming coming out of the emergency exit. It was the sneaky lieutenant trying to surprise us. So to teach him a lesson, I immediately grabbed my weapon and yelled out, "Who goes there?"

As he came out, he shouted out, "Do not shoot! It is me, the lieutenant!"

I said, "That was stupid and dangerous."

I think he learned something that day: do not be a sneak because you could get yourself shot.

With all the security, it was alarming the amount of thievery that we encountered. However, other countries that had units around the area—many of them did not even have fences—were hardly ever robbed. Then I found out their secret; they would literally hang thieves by their thumbs and put them on display. This is what I call "show and see" and not what we call "politically correct."

Now that I would be leaving in a few weeks, I was worried something would happen. When I first arrived, it was a strange feeling that I had. It was hard to explain, this feeling of emptiness. Then, I did not even care, thinking I would never see home again.

We found out there was an attack on one of the outposts near the demilitarized zone, which left a fatality of one of the radio operators. There were other ambushes; none of it ever made any news back home. It is astounding how times have changed; today, if someone drops a statement, it is heard around the world.

I could not believe how fast these last thirteen months had flown. I had seen a lifetime of poverty and sickness. Even in the darkest days, nothing is greater than this country of ours. One should never take our country or freedom and way of life for granted.

I found it difficult saying good-bye to my new friends, knowing I would never see them again. I especially would miss little Park. He kept saying, "Do not leave," in his broken English, leaving both of us in tears. I tried to stay in touch, but being so far away, it became impossible.

I went to Tokyo, Japan, for a flight back to the States. I was still in no real hurry to get back. I was able to stay in Tokyo for as long as I wanted. I reported to the separation section and just said I wanted to stay another day, and no questions were asked. I was staying at a military base where they fed and housed me.

I did some sightseeing and saw some areas that were in ruins from the bombing during World War II.

I did not stay long mainly because some of the natives literally spit on me, and I could hear nothing but negative remarks. So I decided to cut this visit short and make arrangements for the next flight out.

Going home was a lot more enjoyable. I flew direct on a commercial flight. I left Japan at 7:00 in the evening and arrived in the States the same night, because of the time difference.

When I got back to the continental United States—we landed in Oakland, California—the first thought I had was to kiss the ground. Hours later, I flew home to the East Coast.

Chapter 13

Back to Reality

I got a warm reception from my family and friends. For the first few days, I just slept like a baby. I was scheduled to report to Fort Meade in Maryland for my new assignment in about a week.

Mom was so happy that I had come back in one piece she went to the extreme to have it announced on the Greek radio stations. The phone did not stop ringing.

My car required too much money to repair, and my brother Harry was buying a new car, so he gave me his old one. It was a 1954 Desoto, and he told me it ran fairly well. It just had one problem: it leaked brake fluid. He kept a gallon of it in the trunk. I just had to remember every so often to fill it. He also said once in a while, the push-button for the automatic transmission fell off.

We had cousins living in Baltimore, so Mom came for the ride with me to spend a few days with them. The ride down to Baltimore went well. I dropped Mom off and then drove to my new unit to check in and get myself situated.

I was not scheduled to report until 800 hours the next morning. I went back to my cousin's, had dinner, and hung around a while. As I was leaving, Mom said, "Be careful." I had to remind her I had just come back from thirteen months of hell. I guess mothers will always worry.

I was on the Baltimore/Washington expressway getting ready to exit when I realized I had no brakes. This was no time to forget about the brake fluid. I took the curve at a relatively high speed, and I could hear the tires squeal. I was lucky this car was built like a tank.

The road was slightly hilly, which helped to slow the car down. I could see a traffic light at a distance. It was red. I knew I had to stop somehow. I tried the parking brakes (emergency). That helped somewhat, but I was still moving at a good speed. I dropped the car into neutral and then into low gear, and the transmission button fell off. I turned off the ignition, took a deep breath, held the steering wheel as tight as I could, and then I headed for a tree where I came to a dead stop.

I made sure I was all right. It was extremely dark. The only light I had was the headlight. I must have spilled more brake fluid than I could get into the small hole. Now I had to find the button, which had fallen off, and without any light, it was no joke. I finally found it and put it back. I headed back to my unit without any other problems.

The next morning, I checked the car; the bumper had a slight dent. As for me, that was a different story. I was one giant sore. After that incident, I would make sure I checked the brake fluid daily.

My first day was a piece of cake. All I did was look busy and answer the phone. Most of the unit was out on a training assessment. I was getting many phone calls about different situations; some I tried to answer, others I just took messages about.

This one girl was calling and asking for a certain individual. I told her all the guys were out on a training assessment and would not be back until late that night.

She apparently did not believe me because she kept calling back. Before I knew it, I had started making conversation with her, and then I had her phone number. Later that night, the unit pulled in from their training mission.

This enormous fellow came into the office, told me his name, and asked if he had any messages. When I saw the size of his arms, he made me feel like a ninety-pound weakling. I told him some girl kept calling. I was glad I never gave her my real name.

I got to meet most of the fellows, and they told me that the big guy was a nut and not to get on his bad side. We became friends, and he wanted me to meet his girlfriend.

I was a little uncomfortable about meeting her. I keep putting it off as long as I could. One Friday, just before I was to leave, he got my attention and said, "I want you to meet someone." Sure enough, it was his girlfriend; she had come to pick him up. I had no choice but to meet her.

When he introduced me to her, she asked, "Do I know you? Because your voice sounds remarkably familiar."

I tried to keep the conversation to a minimum. Then she went on with all these questions, and I was trying to cut her short. Then he said, "Why not join us?"

I thanked them and said I had other plans made, but maybe another time.

I later found out she was a dancer in one of the clubs in Baltimore. I made sure I stayed far away from that club.

Many times, a few of us would drive into the city of Baltimore to some of the local bars and clubs. Sometimes we would even wear the dress uniforms just to attract some girls. There was this one time when this bartender read my name tag. He said to me, "Are you related to Milt Pappas, the pitcher for the Baltimore Orioles?"

I replied, "What? My brother?"

Before I could tell him I was kidding, he shouted out, "Free drinks for you and your friends!" So as not to hurt his feelings, I kept my mouth shut; we enjoyed the free drinks.

This one night, we went club hopping. I was trying to avoid the club my friend's girl worked at. It had to be well past midnight when we hit the last club. I realized it was the same club, and I was telling the guys, "Let's skip this spot and go back to the unit." I was outnumbered, so I had no choice. I kept my distance from the stage where the girls were performing.

I was at the bar nursing my drink when all of a sudden this girl tapped my shoulder and said, "Hi, I'm glad you came."

I was speechless. She said, "Stick around. I am next to dance."

I told the guys, "Guess who is dancing next." I told them it was our crazy friend's girl. Big mistake. Now they wanted to stay. I had to admit she was very hot and sexy, but to stay healthy, I avoided her. They must have thought I was crazy not to stay and see her performance. I never told anybody about the telephone conversation. Was I being too unadventurous?

The next day, her boyfriend said to me, "I heard you went to see my girl dancing. What did you think?"

To keep the peace, I just said what I had to.

Once in a while, on a hot summer night, we would pack the car and go to a drive-in movie. We would all chip in and buy a few six-packs and snacks and enjoy the movie.

The fellow who owned the car we all went in said in a serious manner, "I have a splendid suggestion. I'll hide in the trunk and use that money I would spend on admission and get another six-pack."

I said, "Are you crazy?"

He was serious, and he went through with it.

Just before we got to the drive-in, he jumped into the trunk, and we slammed it shut. The guy who was driving asked, "Where is the key?"

The guy in the trunk shouted, "I got them!"

Here, it was, 80 degrees plus, and he was in the trunk. All we could do was remove the back seat and tear a hole, so he could pass the key out. I said, "Was this all worth it?"

He replied, "Oh yes, anything for a six-pack."

I would drive into Baltimore to see my cousin, and it would mean a home-cooked meal. So it was well worth the trip. Her daughter Maria lived with her; she was a few years younger than I. She introduced me to some of her older girlfriends.

I got friendly with one of her friends, and we hit it off pretty decently. We saw each other quite a bit. I was not looking for any long commitments at this time, but she was. So I became the bad guy and stopped seeing her.

My godmother lived in a suburban town outside of Washington DC called Rockville, Maryland, so on occasion, I would visit her family. So between visiting her and my cousin and sometimes going home, I stayed busy socially.

The car's transmission was acting up. I was thinking of the incident I had had earlier. One of the guys told me to put some sawdust into the transmission, where the fluid went. I had nothing to lose but had no clue if it would work or how long it would run, so I just took my chances. It ran great, so I hoped it would last until I finished up my time. I would never attempt to drive home, so whenever I went home, I took the train or bus.

My cousin asked me to take her shopping. She was always good to me. How could I say no? Everything was going smoothly. I came to a red light; after the light turned green, I proceeded to go. All I got was a racing engine; the forward gear was not responding.

After trying it again, I realized the transmission had had it. So I thought to myself, "Let me try reverse." I crossed my fingers; I then put the car in reverse. The car made a clicking sound and started moving.

I was not too far from her house. So I drove the car slowly backward to the house. My cousin was getting extremely nervous and concerned. She said to me in Greek, "What is happening?" I told her everything was under control, and I continued to drive the car in reverse.

When we got back to the house, she quickly got out of the car doing the sign of the cross. I tried to explain the car had broken down, that it was no longer drivable.

I still had a few months to go, which made it extremely inconvenient. I was a true believer that everything that happened in life happened for a reason.

Chapter 14

Payback

While I was in Korea, my ex-fiancée and I had a joint account. More than half of my military pay was going to the account. Then I found out she had cleaned out the account. I immediately had them stop taking money from my salary, and she had the nerve to get upset.

I had some leave days owed me, so I went home for a week. I was determined to get my money no matter what I had to do. I had planned a way to win her back.

I made it a point to surprise her when she got out of work. I knew her weak points and took advantage. This went on for a couple of days, and she finally gave in and went for a drink. We saw each other for the rest of the week.

As much as I hated taking the train or bus, I had no choice if I wanted to succeed with my plans. This went on for a few weekends; we had told nobody.

After a while, my friends and family must have found out I was seeing her. They called me crazy and told me that she was not worth it. I told them I was not seeing her. I realized I could not take any chances if I wanted to succeed with my plan.

I had no car to get around, and I knew she hated that. She was so spoiled that she had always wanted door service in the past. I told her I could not afford a car at this time. She said she would help by paying the down payment, which was about the amount she had taken from the account.

She then broke down and told me everything; she was seeing a friend I had made while in basic training. I was holding a glass when she told me, and I literally broke the glass in my hand when she said it. This came like a shock;

he had stayed Stateside after we completed training. Here, I was trying to be the good guy, and she was being a naughty girl.

While I was cleaning the blood off my hand, she apologized for being stupid and sending me a Dear John letter and taking all the money out of the savings. She said she still loved me. I had to bite my tongue. I had to keep on track, so I told her that I forgave her, I understood what she had gone through, and I still loved her.

I still had some leave time coming, and this was all part of my plan. So I took the opportunity to take advantage. Everything was falling in place. So we went together to look for a new car at the Don Allen dealership just off Columbus Circle. We both saw this beautiful brand-new 1964 sliver-blue two-door hardtop Chevy Impala.

The car was not even on the road yet, but because I was in the military, they let me have it before it was available to the public. She loved it as much as I did, so it made it that much easier. She signed her name on some papers, and I made her feel that the car was also under her name. The registration and ownership was just under my name.

They told us it would take until the next day for the paperwork to be completed. So I told her we would go tomorrow after lunch to pick the car up; everything was falling in place.

The next day, bright and early, I picked up the car and went to my own bank and refinanced the car under just my name.

I wrote her a "Dear Mary" letter. As bad as I felt doing it, I just thought back to when I was halfway around the world and what she did. I could have been a real bitch and taken and did more, but I just wanted back what she took. The old saying is, "Paybacks are a bitch."

I told my family the whole story now that I had accomplished my goal. Everybody thought I was crazy for going back with her. They could now understand that I was not crazy but just being "slick like a fox." I asked them, "Do you think I could live with, much less marry, a person like that, knowing she may do it again?"

I felt sorry for my mother; this was a vital lesson for her. She had accepted her from day one because she was Greek. Her other daughters-in-law, because they were not Greek, were never welcomed that easily, and they turned out to be just like family. Mom realized it was not where they were from, but what they were that mattered, and also that one was never too old to learn.

My new car had a new slick look. It had style, which caught everybody's eye. A few days later, I drove my new car back to the army base with a strong feeling of satisfaction and accomplishment.

I was enjoying my new set of wheels. While I was driving, a state trooper flagged me to stop. "I hope you do not mind," he said, "but your car caught my attention, and I had to take a closer look."

All my friends at the base were teasing me, asking where I found the money for a new car. I told them some girl had bought it for me. Little did they know …

Now that I had a car, I could get around again without being a burden to others. I would drive home when I had a long weekend. I was not one for picking up hitchhikers. The only time I would ever do it was when it was for individuals in uniform. I knew the feeling of trying to get around without a set of wheels.

My time was winding down, and soon, I would be a civilian again. I made it a point to thank my cousin and my godmother for all the outstanding meals and enjoyable times. Most of the fellows I became friends with were from the West Coast or the Midwest; I knew most likely I would never see them again.

Chapter 15

New Changes

I got my release from active duty on Friday 13, just before the holidays. The number 13 was going to be a lucky number; I could just feel it. When I got out of the service, I took a short vacation and went back to my old job.

I thought after two years of active duty, I would be totally done. Boy was I wrong. I had to complete two years of reserve duty. My obligation was two weeks in the summer, plus one night each week.

I had no girlfriend to worry about, so it was like a night out. I came across some of the fellows I had not seen since basic training. We traded some stories and experiences, and we would sometimes stop and have a few beers.

I needed to purchase new clothing. Throughout most of my younger years, I had always been on the thin side, even while I was in the service. I decided to buy a tailor-made suit. When I went to pick up my suit a few weeks later, to my surprise, it was too tight around the waist. I could not believe that within that short period I had gained that much. Was it Mom's home cooking?

One of my friends also finished his tour of duty. He had spent his time in Vietnam and got wounded, not once, but twice. We found out soon thereafter that he died in a motorcycle accident; I always said God works in mysterious ways.

I was dating, but I still felt bitter about my last romance. I would label every girl I was seeing, which I realized was not being fair. I quit dating for a short period to try to get some of the bitterness out of my system.

One night, while I was heading home on Harlem River Drive, I saw red lights flashing through my rearview mirror, so I pulled over. I noticed this large African-American police officer walking slowly toward the car. I rolled down my window. He shouted to me, "License and registration." He hesitated and said, "Pappas. Did you go to…" Again he hesitated, and then he said, "I do not believe it! Mike Pappas?"

I took a closer look and noticed it was my friend from high school. I got out. With traffic whizzing past us, we gave each other a high five and a hug. If anybody was watching this, it had to have looked funny.

We chatted for a while before his partner called him. We exchanged phone numbers, and he said, "Be sure to call, or I will give you that ticket."

He invited me to his home in Brooklyn where I got to meet his wife and kids. While we were talking about the school days and politics, he said I should apply for the police academy. I laughed. "Are you joking?"

He had been on the force about three years, all because a friend of his had talked him into it. He said, "I will get an application."

I had never given it much thought before. It was something I had to seriously think over. I spoke to some other friends. Some said I was crazy, and others thought it was a decent career choice. So after a few weeks, I filled the application out and gave it back to him. I had missed the examination for this cycle. I told my mother about it, and she made the sign of the cross and said to me, *"Eacer thelus"?* (Are you crazy?).

One Sunday, while I was attending church, I came across an old friend whom I had not seen since I went into the service. We chatted for a while; she invited me to her church group for a social get-together. She went on and said, "There are plenty of single girls."

I got a letter from the police academy that I had to report for my exam. I told my mother again, and again she yelled at me and called me stupid. As much as she was against it, I reported for the exam as scheduled.

The night after I took the exam, I went down to the social club at the church. My friend greeted me and introduced me to some people. I met a lot of girls that night, but only one of them stood out. Little did I know, the girl I met I would marry years later. While I was talking with her, I teased her because she was wearing an eye patch. I called her Captain Hook. She did not like my comment, and she cut me short.

Later I apologized to her, and she told me her name was Moska; even though I was Greek, I had never heard of that name. I loved her name and found out it meant "a fragrance".

I ran into her again at a dance, and we hit it off. We danced and spoke for most of the evening. Apparently, she had been checking around about me. I knew because she asked me if I was the same guy who had just returned from Korea and had left his girlfriend for a Korean girl.

I was somewhat taken by surprise, only because I had never mentioned to anyone outside of my family what had happened. It turned out that one of her friends was friendly with my ex-fiancée. I explained to her what had happened. The truth was that my ex had sent me a "Dear John" letter just before the Christmas holiday. Then to add salt to the wound, she was seeing an army buddy of mine from basic training.

At first, she seemed to have mixed emotions. In a way, I could not blame her; after all, we had just met. Except for this minor setback, I thought we had hit it off pretty decently.

After we had dated, I told her I was waiting for my test results on becoming a New York City police officer. She gave me the impression that she was not too thrilled about it. So I kept quiet about it until I got my results.

I told my mother I had met a lovely Greek girl; she seemed happy about it. She was a little hesitant about it because of my previous experience. Then she started interrogating me like only a mother could; she went on to ask which section of Greece. When I told her she was from one of the twelve islands, she got really excited, because they were from the same area. Mom wanted to meet her; I told her I was just getting to know her. "Give me a little while and you can meet the whole family."

When I first met Moska, she was like a breath of fresh air and came across like no other girl I had dated. I wanted a girl who would appreciate anything I did, large or small, expensive or inexpensive. I came to discover that Moska was that girl; when we dated, she never demanded anything and appreciated everything.

I remember on one of the dates, we took the Staten Island ferry and made a night of it. She never made any negative remarks. I was thinking to myself she probably thought I was a cheapskate.

Another time, we had gone to a diner for a late snack. We just parked the car and as we were walking toward the entrance, this car was coming toward us slowly. It was then when we realized that there was no driver. The car was heading straight for the main intersection.

Moska got a little nervous when she saw me chasing the car and said, "Be careful." She must have been thinking, *What a nut I met!* While I was I chasing the car, I noticed the door was open. I jumped in and hit the brakes just before it went into traffic. Call me a nut, but at that moment, my reaction was to try to stop the car and hopefully avoid a horrible accident.

We went in and reported the incident to management, and we came to find out it belonged to an off-duty policeman. I did not even get a thank-you. Maybe I should have minded my own business.

I remember Dad telling me about the World's Fair back in 1939. Twenty-five years later, they had it again at the same location on 1,300 acres in Flushing Meadows Park in Queens. The fair opened in 1964 and closed in 1965.

Moska and I went. It was something to see and remember. We saw things then that were just visions at the time. Now some of them are a reality. The old saying went, "Meet you at the World's Fair." That was so true, because we both met so many people.

I took on another job working part-time at night at a restaurant called Long-champs, as a food checker. I only worked a few days a week, so as not to conflict with school.

I received the results from my police exam. I first told my mother about passing the test. She came down real hard on me; she could not believe that I was still seriously going through with it.

I invited Moska for dinner to show her off where I had started working. I was starting to get serious with her, and now I had to tell the new girl in my life about my career change.

After dinner, I broke the news that I had passed the police exam and was waiting for my background check to be completed. She replied in a firm voice that if I went through with it, she would stop seeing me. I was somewhat upset with her comment. I did not answer or even say one word. In fact, I changed the subject.

She asked me to take her home. While we were driving, neither of us said one word. I did not want to say something I would regret. When we got to her house, I started looking for a parking spot. She opened the door and said, "Do not bother calling me if you go through with it."

I guess my Greek pride got the best of me, and I said, "Okay." I left and drove home. I was hoping to make a career change and now this. It was bad enough my mother was against it and now Moska, too.

I had made friends with my boss Jack, and we became close. I told him that I had passed the police academy exam. I was to start the academy shortly, but I had two problems. I told him about my mother and my new girlfriend.

He said that it was a tough call, and only I could make that decision. He said, "Think about it carefully, and whatever it is, I'm sure it will be for the best." He also said if I was serious with her, I might someday live with her, so I should think about it.

I was scheduled to start the academy in a few weeks. This made it even that much more difficult, because I was ready to give my notice at work, but now I had second thoughts.

After carefully weighing out all my options, and between my mother and Moska beating me up about it, I decided not to proceed any further with my police career.

I called Moska and told her I wanted to see her and that it was vital. So

I drove up to her house. I told her I was not going through with it. She was extremely pleased to hear that, and she gave me a giant hug.

I had just one question: "Why were you so against it?" She told me that her ex had been a police officer, and she did not want to go through that experience again.

When I told my mother, she replied, "I see you found your "marlowe" (brains.)

Her parents were extremely strict in many ways, especially about whom she dated. Her parents were just like my mother; they were from the old school, and nothing would change their feelings.

I got to meet her family. Her brother worked in a local deli in Midtown Manhattan. He told me he was opening his own deli. I wished him much success with his new enterprise.

Mom finally got to meet Moska's family. She invited them all to the house for a Sunday dinner. Her brother could not come because he had just opened his new deli.

Our mothers hit it off, and they eventually became more like sisters. Mom said, "Do not let her get away."

I teased her about it, and I said, "Remember what happened before?"

She said, "I can tell because of her parents."

If there is only one thing I learned after all these years, it was not to second-guess your parents, especially your mother.

Her parents seemed to appreciate me. I'm sure being Greek helped. After we had dated a few months, her father approached me and asked me, "What are your intentions?"

I was somewhat taken by surprise, but knowing how Greek parents were, I was not totally surprised, so I quickly replied that they were honorable.

I told him that we were going steady. Her father continued to ask me about the relationship, so I had to remind him that we were in America, not Greece. I told him that my feelings were true. We had only just started seeing each other, and marriage was forever.

That seemed to put him on hold for a few more months. Then he started again and reminded me if I wanted to continue to see his daughter, he wanted to see a ring on her finger. I told him to be patient; it was just a matter of time.

I started seriously looking for a diamond ring at different jewelry stores. Then, I remembered one of the merchants that I had made friends with years earlier; he told me if ever I wanted to purchase any precious stones, I should see him.

After we had dated for ten months, we got engaged. I told her father I was giving her the ring at dinner that night. He said, "I will believe it when I see it on her finger."

I wanted it to be an evening she would never forget. I took her to a French restaurant on Fifth Avenue right across from Central Park.

It was a glorious evening. I wanted to surprise her when I gave her the ring. When the waiter brought us the drinks, I managed to slip the ring into her drink. My biggest concern was that she would swallow it. I could still remember the gleam in her eyes when she saw it.

Both her parents were so thrilled and excited, especially her father. He told us that he was going to give us an engagement party. In all that time, I had never seen her father with so much joy.

Moska called me Monday morning at work to tell me that her father had had a fatal heart attack. I had just seen him Saturday night. He looked and felt okay and was so excited. Perhaps he had died of sheer happiness. So now we had to wait at least a year to get married out of respect for her family. I felt sorry because of her father's loss, mainly because she would have been the first one to get married.

With the passing of her dad, things were not the same for quite a while. We just took one day at a time.

We had many power failures throughout the years, but I will always remember the one on November 9, 1965. I was just leaving work, and a bunch of us were getting off the elevator when the power went out just after 5:00 p.m. We thought it was just a temporary power loss, until we found out it was the whole city.

Traffic became a nightmare with no traffic lights. A few of us decided to stop at one of the restaurants, until the power came back. I tried calling home with no luck. We had something to eat. After a few hours, I realized the power was not coming on anytime soon. I decided to walk home because traffic was at a standstill. It was a strange feeling walking home; the only lights were the vehicles and the flashlights people were carrying. I saw so many people partying as I was passing different bars.

When I got home, Mom was cooking all the food in the refrigerator because she was of afraid of it spoiling. With nothing else to do, I went to bed. The next morning, the lights started coming on slowly throughout the city. Millions of people were in the dark from New Jersey up to Ontario, Canada, for more than twelve hours.

It is not till we lose something like electricity that we realize how we take things for granted. What is one to do without it? On the positive side, nine months later, more babies came into the world.

I was still doing my one night of reserve duty, plus it was just about time to put in my two weeks. Moska was not too thrilled about it, but she knew it was out of our hands. Uncle Sam had me for about another year.

The two weeks seemed to fly by, and it felt terrific to get back to civilian life and start making arrangements for the wedding.

A few months before we were to get married, I had already committed myself to being best man for my friend Gregg. To top it off, I was also going to be a godfather for my boss's daughter. Both my mother and Moska said I should decline; they felt it was too much in a short time. I felt obligated, and besides, deep down, I wanted to do it.

In spite of everything, all went well with both occasions, and they both thanked me for doing it, knowing that I was getting married in a few months. Now we just focused on the momentous day, getting the last-minute details.

When we were deciding on the bridal party, everything went well except when I was going to pick my best man. Mom got involved and said I must ask both my godmother and godfather to be my best man. I was slightly upset about it because I had different plans.

She went on to say, "It is customary to have your godparents do it. If you do not ask them, it is shameful." Mom knew how to make me feel guilty.

Again, I knew not to argue with Greek tradition, so I just bit my tongue.

I just knew the number 13 was going to be good luck, because we got married on November 13. We were married in the church in which I had I grown up. The priest who performed the ceremony was new; this would be his first wedding since he had been ordained a priest.

To make it even more unique, his name was Father Pappas.

We had our honeymoon in beautiful Puerto Rico and St. Thomas. We had gone first class and stayed at top hotels; we spared nothing, because if we did not do it now, we might never do it again. This was Moska's first time flying ever, and to top it off, we flew on a helicopter from the Pan Am building to the Kennedy airport.

We flew right over my old neighborhood. That was a sight I will always remember. I teased Moska and told her I could see my mother hanging clothes on the roof. The flight was under ten minutes, and there was no traffic.

She was still nervous about going on the airplane even after the flight on the helicopter. I told her it was a lot safer than driving. Somehow, she did not buy it. Going first class made her feel a little more comfortable, so I'm glad that part worked out. We arrived in Puerto Rico in a few hours, and she was in her glories.

My friend's son was living in Puerto Rico, and he showed us sights on the island the average person would never see. After a few days, we flew on to St. Thomas on a small plane. I will never forget it flew so low over the water we could see the sharks smiling. It was not a long flight, but it seemed forever, especially for Moska.

St. Thomas was breathtaking, and the view from the top of the mountain was out of a book. The guide told us he had to come down from the mountain when the sun started to set. He claimed his blood was too thin to withstand when the temperature would fall below 70 degrees. I told him, "Don't ever come to New Jersey in the winter."

Neither of us were serious drinkers, but after tasting a drink in St. Thomas called a piña colada, we got hooked. When we got home, one would think we were lushes; that's how much we enjoyed this new drink. There were times they did not believe Moska's age, and the sad part was she had no ID. We sometimes had to order room service to have a drink together.

Chapter 16

A New Lifestyle

When we got back, we made our home in a town called Teaneck, New Jersey. A few months later, one of the small planes that had taken us from Puerto Rico to St. Thomas crashed with no survivors. Moska's first remark was, "I'm not flying for a long, long time."

Years later, the same helicopter we took to the airport had a horrible accident that killed five people. It seems that the landing gear was broken, and with rotors still turning, it tipped over. Four people who were outside the helicopter waiting to board were killed. It was also reported that part of a rotor blade broke off and sailed over the side of the building, killing a pedestrian on the street below. Two other people were seriously hurt. Talk about being in the wrong place!

When Moska heard this, her casual comment was, "I'm definitely not flying especially on a helicopter."

When we first got married, Moska would iron my socks and underwear, just like my mother did. Now I ask, how many guys can honestly say that? Unfortunately, that did not last.

Being married was fun, and we would do things together, even food shopping. We would buy all the meats where Harry worked. He would cut the meat just like a traditional butcher shop. He was always telling us funny stories about certain customers.

I received a promotion at my job to sales coordinator, and I got a delightful raise and my own desk. I also did a little local traveling.

Mom would get mad because she claimed I did not call her enough. I tried to explain that between work and my new life, I was very busy it was not that I did not think about her. The problem was I let one issue lead to another.

Then she went on to say, "Remember, I will not be around forever." She was entirely correct, so I tried to make it a habit to call her more often. Moska also came to the rescue, and she would call both our moms. Mom would constantly say, "Wait till you have children of your own, and then you will understand."

Come summer, before I could even take a vacation, I had to complete my two weeks of reserve duty. Moska never enjoyed it when I had to go for the week. The happy news was this was going to be my last two weeks; I would be getting my discharge from active duty.

For our first anniversary, we drove down to Miami Beach, mainly because Moska was not ready to fly just yet. We stopped in Virginia Beach to see her cousins and take a short break from all the driving. After spending a few days there, we continued to the sunny state of Florida.

When we got to Florida, there was a sign with a picture of Jackie Gleason saying, "Welcome to the Sunshine State. Only eight hours to Miami Beach." That was a shot in the arm. The only unfortunate part of the trip was that Moska did not drive; living in the city, she did not need a car, so she never got a driver's license. I told her, "The first thing you must do when we get back home is get your license."

When we got back, I needed a vacation from all the driving. A few months later, Moska was not feeling well. The happy news was she was expecting. She stopped working about eight months into her pregnancy. I told her I wanted her to be a stay-at-home mother, even if I had to get a second job.

We were blessed with a son that we named Charles, out of respect for her father. Normally, with the old Greek tradition, you named your firstborn from the father's side. Mom already had a grandson John. Moska's mother was especially happy, because this was her first grandchild.

Moska finally got her driver's license, which made things that much easier for both of us. Just for the record, she went to a driving school. We purchased another car; now she did not have to depend on me.

Shortly after Charles came into this world, there was a sad event; an African-American clergyman named Martin Luther King Junior was assassinated. I had heard about him in the news of civil rights marches; his biggest dream was peace and love. This had brought some memories back of when Gregg and I traveled to the South.

I found it hard to believe that some people were still living with this hate and bitterness. This was another time Mom would say we lived in a "fake world"; it was times like this that I knew what she actually meant.

I received word that my company was moving to Connecticut. I enjoyed my job, but to move out of state? I was not ready for that change just yet.

When my brother-in-law discovered what was happening, he approached me with an offer. "Why not come into business with me?"

I said, "You're crazy. I have no experience." I could not tell salami from bologna. Besides that, I did not have enough money at this time to invest. He said we would work it out. I thanked him for the proposal, but a change like that I had to discuss with Moska.

Mom called me to tell me my friend Teddy was home on leave, and he wanted to see me. I called Moska to tell her I would be home late and that I wanted to spend a little time with my friend Teddy, who was home on leave.

I met him at my mother's house; it was sure great to see him. We went for a few drinks, and we spoke about the earlier years, and all the fun and crazy things we did.

He told me he was scheduled to be released from active duty in less than five months. I could feel something was bothering him. Then he hit me with the news that he was going to Vietnam. I was in total shock. I said, "With so little time left, why is Uncle Sam sending you there?"

I said to him in an extremely upset manner, "You must get an exemption from going."

He said he had already applied for it, but by the time Uncle Sam reviewed it, he would be heading home. He was even thinking about not reporting for his re-deployment. I told him that was a tough call, and it was one only he could make. Before we both drank one too many, we called it a night. We hugged each other, and I wished him a safe trip back.

Not even two months later, his family told us he was killed in action. The report was his unit was ambushed while on patrol; the fellows behind him witnessed it but survived the attack without a scratch.

I could not help thinking about what he had said to me before he left. All I could say was, "God works in mysterious ways."

He came to America at a young age to start a new life and died at the age of twenty-three. I could not help thinking of the fun few years we had growing up. What a waste of a life—and thousands of other lives—for a war that I felt we should never have gotten into, because of the way we fought and ended it.

His funeral was one of the biggest ones I ever attended. We all lost a dear friend that day. I loved him like a brother, and his memory is always with me.

Mom had gotten notice that the apartment house was going to be torn down. After all these years, they were making room for a luxury garden high-rise apartment building. It was another heartbreaking time.

Mom moved out to Sunnyside in Queens. It took awhile for her to adjust. As it is many times, it was never the same.

Mary was dating a lot of guys, like doctors and lawyers. When she finally got married, she settled for a part-time jeweler and musician. I think Mary was taken more by the fact that he played an instrument called a bouzouki and was a jeweler. His name was John; he played for a well-known Greek band.

My brother-in-law invited me for lunch at his new deli. He then brought up the business proposal again. I told him I was still discussing it with his sister and I would make a decision really soon.

The offer sounded decent, but I had to look for a job that I felt comfortable with. I was not having any luck. I was either overqualified, or the money was not there. With Moska not working, I could not afford to be out of work for any amount of time. Now the offer started to look even better.

I kept thinking about what Moska had said to me: that I would regret it. She became even more anxious and extremely loud. She said, "Your ideas are extremely different from my brother's," and we continued to argue on the subject.

With time winding down, with no luck, and with the thought of the money, I did not listen to her opinion. So I gave my two weeks' notice and started an entirely different lifestyle.

Epilogue

Everything in this book is what I experienced as I was growing up. There might be other facts. These are the ones I remembered.

Ask anyone who grew up in that era, as tough as life was, it was a time we will never forget. No one ever worried where the car keys were because they were always in the car, and the doors were never locked. You got your gas pumped, windshield cleaned, and oil checked without asking. Plus, you did not pay for air. Jar and bottle items did not need safety caps. A weapon in school meant a slingshot. You played sports without adult supervision. Fearing for our lives meant fear of getting the strap whenever we got out of line.

Life is a learning experience from the first day you come into this world. As much as you cannot change the past, you can sure still change the future and do whatever you want.

Remember, if something sounds too good, question it!

Family values are the backbone of our upbringing, then, now, and tomorrow. Live every day to its fullest and enjoy it as if it were your last day, because you never know what tomorrow might bring.